I0532780

Un*think*able

Taking the hand of Jesus
Through Pain and Suffering into a
Life of Freedom and Purpose

HEATHER BRADLEY

Unthinkable: Taking the hand of Jesus through pain and suffering into a life of freedom and purpose.
By Heather Bradley
Published by Selfpublishing.com
Austin, TX (State Abbrev.) #####
Copyright © 2024 Heather Bradley

Cover design by Joice Panilagao

ISBN Paperback: 979-8-89316-9-584
ISBN Ebook: 979-8-89316-9-591

DEDICATION

To Jesus Christ my Lord and Savior. You are my breath, my life, and my everything. Without you nothing matters. With you all things come together. I love you—also thank you for being my friend.

Therefore we do not lose heart. Though outwardly we are wasting away, yet inwardly we are being renewed day by day. For our light and momentary troubles are achieving for us an eternal glory that far outweighs them all. So we fix our eyes not on what is seen, but on what is unseen, since what is seen is temporary, but what is unseen is eternal.

2 Corinthians 4:16–18

WANT TO GO DEEPER?

If you are reading this book with friends make sure you get your copy of the Discussion Guide to go with your book study. You can get this free guide delivered to your email! Simply visit the website below and fill out the form. Put the word unthinkable in your subject line.

Get your copy by visiting:
www.truthfreedomministry.com/unthinkable

CONTENTS

INTRODUCTION

*"An arrow can only be shot by pulling it backwards.
When life is dragging you back with difficulties, just
imagine it's going to launch you into something great."*
~ Paulo Coelho

Have you ever found yourself in the middle of an unthinkable situation? One that left you feeling undone? The rug was pulled out from underneath you, and there was nothing left to stand on? We often see tragedies on the nightly news or hear people's unthinkable stories on talk shows. We may even know someone who walked through a horrible circumstance. The truth is, we tend to think that these experiences could only happen to someone else.

But what happens when we become the someone else? It's hard to wrap our minds around something unthinkable happening to us. We can't picture ourselves as a character in one of these stories. We tell ourselves there is no way we could survive it—that it is beyond our ability and capacity. We may even begin to question who God is and how He could allow these things to happen.

Where do we go when we find ourselves smack-dab in the middle of one of these stories? A story we never asked to be a part of? A character we never asked to play? Suddenly, everything we thought we knew about life does not make sense anymore.

When it happened to me, I found myself in an unthinkable story. The tragedy had the ability to flatline me and change the course of my life forever. I had a choice to make. I could turn away from God and become a victim of my circumstance, or I could reach for the extended hand of my Savior and be pulled into something more. Did my painful story change me? Yes, there was no way *around it*, but there was a way *through it* that would bring true healing, and the way was named Jesus.

Now, let me ask you a question? Where are you today in your "unthinkable" story? Are you reeling from the fresh pain that just struck, or are you in the middle of your journey when heartache feels like your new norm? Did you find yourself picking up this book looking for a lifeline? Maybe you feel stuck and don't know where to go from here. We can feel so hopeless and desperate no matter where we are in the story. The tentacles of hurt, fear, pain, hopelessness can wrap us so tight that there appears to be no way of escape. I wanted more to come from my story, and right there in the thick of it was Jesus inviting me into His story. He wants to invite you too.

What if I told you there is hope in tragedy and that you don't have to stay stuck in this story forever? What if I told you there is a way out of the pain to the other side—where hope, peace, freedom, and healing break through? What if I told you I know the answer to the pain from the situation that has knocked the life out of you? What if I told you that you could breathe again and laugh again? What if I told you that you could find purpose in your pain?

I love diving into analogies; God often uses them to speak to me. I like to consider it our special language together. For example, I have an arrow-shaped bracelet I wear, and right above my writing desk, there's an arrow in the middle of a bunch of pictures. When I'm writing, I can't help but glance up and think about what an arrow represents in my life. First and most simply, it reminds me to be directed toward the path pointing to Jesus.

But there is another analogy about an arrow that I want you to grasp. It's one where we are like arrows being catapulted into the earth with purpose and precision. We are partners with Jesus—a master archer—to bring the kingdom of God to this dark world where pain and suffering run rampant. We can only be precision arrows when we allow Jesus to heal us from our own painful stories. We can then become arrows that gain momentum and perfect direction. Can you see how our stories then start to have purpose?

When we find ourselves being pulled back—in this momentary pause before release—we can find our healing in Jesus. Why is the arrow pulled back before being sent into the bull's-eye? Why is there a moment of pause before the arrow is let go? It's because the pull back and pause allow the archer to make the adjustments needed to catapult the arrow with great strength and precision into its intended target. If we don't allow the archer to do his job, then the arrow misses its mark. We need to cooperate with the archer in our story. And then we can be perfectly aimed and catapulted into the plans God has for us.

When we are pulled back by the difficulties of life, we must learn to live in the presence of Jesus, being fully healed: mind, body, and emotions. If we are not careful with how we choose to heal and move forward, we can be caught in a web of despair and sidelined by what happened to us. This is exactly what the enemy would like to happen to us. We can be like a precision arrow shot into the purposes of God, or we can be an arrow with its tip broken off and thrown to the ground only to be trampled on.

When I found myself in the middle of a nightmare over twenty plus years ago, it was a moment in time that the enemy was hoping to trap me in—an unthinkable prison of grief never to recover—but Jesus had a different plan for my life.

This is my story of love and loss. Pain and restoration. This is my story of a prodigal coming home to her Father God amid tragedy. No condemnation—just falling into loving arms to carry me through. Arriving stripped down wearing nothing and being clothed in the most beautiful garments one can imagine. This is my story of a mighty God meeting His daughter in the midst of the darkest place I had ever known and covering me with His great light until the darkness was gone. Tasting, experiencing, knowing, and seeing just how beautiful Jesus is and receiving an eternal legacy with an inheritance greater than an earthly legacy to be obtained.

You, too, can experience this great love right where you are. No matter how long you have been in this chapter of your story, feeling like your life is on pause and you don't know how to hit the play button again, our Father God will enter your unthinkable circumstances and rescue you with His great love and compassion. He can restore and redeem any loss. It's His nature to bind up our wounds, to bring healing to our souls, to come alongside us and walk with us through any circumstance we find ourselves in. This is not just putting a Band-Aid on the wound. This is not a crutch to lean on with a limp the rest of our lives. This is us walking hand and hand with God and finding joy, peace, and love today—in the here and now—not someday in heaven waiting to get there. It's hard to even imagine this kind of healing.

Jesus gives us the freedom to go on and be fulfilled and experience a radical love that only He can pour out. He alone turns our ashes into beauty. He alone can bring forth good from what the enemy meant for harm.

You might be wondering, is there any kind of purpose to our suffering and pain? Can God redeem what we've lost? I know it's paradoxical and doesn't make sense, but the answer to these questions is yes! It's a supernatural response, and it's God's nature to walk us through what we experience in this fallen world. I know some of you are stuck in the aftermath of loss and pain, in a cycle of suffering because of what you've experienced. You want to move forward but can't seem to find your way out of the darkness. Trust me, I get it. The desperation to breathe again on your own is real. To find a new normal marked with peace, not pain.

So, why lose another day? Can you pause here and think back to that pivotal moment in your story that has caused this deep pain and heartache? Be honest with yourself about how you have dealt with it. Do you feel stuck, like you can't move forward? Do you feel defined by the loss? What has been stolen from you? I want to introduce you to someone whose presence brings hope. Someone who calms the storm inside us and brings us into wisdom, revelation, and abundant life. Someone who will never let us down or leave us. Someone who is an unshakable firm foundation where we can find hope and joy again. A place where we can see life from a different lens—not our clouded lens but a clear lens that Jesus Himself gives us to wear. His presence wraps us in true healing and peace like nothing else.

This book is for every child of the King who is carrying a spirit of heaviness, who got written into a story they never asked to be a part of, who is stuck in despair and sees no way out, or maybe who is lost in sorrow over what might have been. You may have no idea who Jesus is or what He has for you, but you are suffering—you, too, are welcome to come here and meet Him—He has been waiting for you. I invite you to journey with me through my unthinkable story of loss and suffering and into a relationship with our heavenly Father. I believe we cannot find true healing and peace anywhere else but in Jesus.

Imagine today that your story can change. Imagine yourself carrying beauty instead of ashes, believing there is purpose from your pain, not just grief, loss, and heaviness. If you are tired of the pain, guess what? That's a perfect place for the healing power of Jesus to come and supernaturally exchange what you're carrying for something so much more. We no longer have to be arrows with broken tips. The master archer can restore our purpose and make us stronger than before. He makes us new! He alone can catapult us with great precision into a life of purpose defined by Him and not our circumstances.

We are going to go on a journey together and enter a place of surrendering our pain at the feet of Jesus and grabbing ahold of His extended hand. When we decide to take that first step, we will begin to trade our pain and loss for a life with Jesus. Here is where we will learn to live in His presence, have our mind-sets renewed by His Word, produce abundant fruit in our lives, and live for a greater purpose than just surviving. This step of surrendering our pain into Jesus's capable hands is where we begin to see Jesus bring forth the good from our loss and pain. So, what are you waiting for? Will you join me on this journey? Jesus is waiting for you.

In Him,
Heather

CHAPTER 1

The Catalyst That Changed Everything

*"One of the greatest paradoxical truths about
Christianity is that the greatest adversity
often produces the greatest blessings."*
~ Charles Colton

C an you remember a season in your life when everything seemed to be going your way? For me, thinking back to the years 1998 1999 brings with it a flood of emotions and memories. These years brought a series of wonderful highs and one of the worst lows in my life. Sometimes we have seasons in our life when we feel on top of the world, when all the stars are lining up!

I had come a long way since high school. I had my daughter my senior year in 1992. From that event alone, I decided I would get it together and push forward to the future. My daughter was born two months before my high school graduation. It was just her and I. So, I started college and along the way fell in love and got married right before I turned twenty-one and my daughter turned three. My husband adopted my daughter, as he is the only dad she has ever known. When I walked across the stage at my college graduation with honors, it felt like a pivotal moment in my life—I had made it!

After college I landed my first "real" job. The kind where you are seen as a professional and receive benefits. I had begun my first year of teaching fifth grade. During this year, my husband and I found out we were expecting a baby, we purchased our first home, and I finally bought a brand-new car right off the showroom floor! My little girl would be a big sister. We were finally living the "American dream." Isn't this supposed to be the ultimate goal we all strive for? I for sure thought we had it all indeed, that all the stars were lining up! Funny thing is that sometimes we don't know what we are missing because it's missing!

When the school year ended and my teaching contract was up, I decided not to renew it but instead spend the next year at home with our new baby. This was an exciting time in our lives. My husband even got a promotion at work that covered my salary! Life was looking really good from our vantage point. I found myself turning my time and attention to all things "home." I was nesting and preparing a place for our new baby—things felt good. Once we found out the baby would be a boy, I began decorating his room and reading everything I could before the arrival of his birth. I was filled with anticipation and excitement of things to come. I felt secure and in control. Everything proceeded well and our baby's due date was approaching.

My mom lived about twelve hours away in Corpus Christi, Texas, and set out on the long drive to come to El Paso, Texas, where we lived at the time. She was planning on spending time with me until the baby came and would help with my daughter as well. Crazy enough, the evening she arrived, we were all getting ready for bed and my water broke! A similar story that would happen with my other future pregnancies as well. We joke that I waited to go into labor when all was right in the world—meaning, when my mama had arrived.

I labored through the night, and Brennen James was born on June 10, 1999. To our surprise he was born on his daddy's birthday! He also shares his middle name with his dad too. He was bald and blue-eyed—unlike our other two boys born later with dark eyes and hair. We settled into life with our new baby boy over the next few months, and everything felt right in the world. As we all know, however, seasons change.

Like any proud parent, I kept a calendar of milestones that Brennen reached each month. When he turned four months old, we headed out to our local grocery store to pick up his first baby food, and back then that meant rice cereal. As he rode in his carrier in the grocery cart and did what babies do—smiled and cooed—we gathered up the supplies needed for this monumental moment.

As we settled in at home and I mixed up his first food, he was sitting in his bouncer kicking and laughing. When I put the first bite in his mouth, he immediately scrunched up his face trying to figure out this strange substance. Laughing to myself, I wondered what he was thinking.

Our day of celebration and fun was abruptly interrupted. This October 14, 1999, beautiful fall day quickly turned into one of the darkest days of my life.

As I watched him in his bouncer, he suddenly seemed to be gasping for air to breathe, and this quickly turned to him not breathing. As I found myself on the phone with 911 and administering CPR, I felt as if time had stopped. It seemed to take the ambulance forever to arrive, but I'm sure it was only minutes. Everything from that point on was as if I was watching someone else's life go by in front of me. I was there physically, but it all felt like the scene from a horror movie. The rug had been yanked out from under me, and I had nowhere to stand. My faulty sense of stability and control was gone. I was now a character in a story I had never asked to play.

As the paramedics took over my living room, I helplessly stood by watching my sweet baby boy fight for his life—in the hands of others. We were quickly swept into the ambulance and arrived at the hospital, where I was told to stay in the waiting room of the ER. My husband arrived from work, and we waited for what seemed like hours. Finally, the ER doctor appeared who had been working to revive Brennen. He looked exhausted and concerned. He said Brennen was stable, but this was a very sick little baby.

Brennen had been growing well during his four months, so we were filled with shock and confusion. We were told he had gone into cardiac arrest and had suffered a heart attack. How does a four-month-old have a heart attack anyway? Certainly, these are not words a parent can process. I remember feeling this intense fear come over me—like I was behind a fortified prison wall, and I could find no way out from behind it. I began to tell myself that he would be fine because they now knew what was wrong and could fix it. It was the only way I could move or breathe.

We learned over the next few hours that he had been born with a severe heart defect. This is what led to the heart attack. He had been growing and thriving, so no one knew or would have suspected. This was not typical of babies born with heart issues. They are usually underweight, and he was far from that. I started having intrusive thoughts about all the "what-ifs."

My mind began to wonder about God. Especially about the times when I was a little girl and Jesus made Himself known to me on more than one occasion. From these occasions, I knew God was real. I wasn't doubting whether He was real or not. I had grown up in the church and was told countless Bible stories about who Jesus was. I remember a couple of times as a young girl having the presence of God come upon me like a weighted blanket. I couldn't move, the feeling was so heavy. It wasn't scary. It was like my soul knew it was the presence of God. However, I hadn't been living for

Jesus throughout high school and into my early adult life, and here again, I was doing my own thing. I wondered why at this moment in the hospital engulfed in fear I was thinking about Jesus and all these encounters.

The doctors and nurses spent the next few days trying to stabilize Brennen enough to Life Flight him to a children's hospital in a larger city that specialized in this type of situation. On the third day of watching and waiting for him to improve enough to be moved, I had this amazing moment with him. As he was lying in his little hospital bed, he began to wake up on his own, out of the sedation that kept him calm, and he saw me. He made eye contact with me, and once he heard my voice, he began trying to wiggle his way toward me. He wanted me to pick him up. To hold him and make him feel safe. He seemed agitated because I couldn't pick him up with all the tubes and machines. I put my hand on him and talked to him to comfort him the best I could. He drifted back to sleep, but I knew in that moment he saw me, and that made me feel good. That moment would end up being the last connection I had with him like that.

The next day, October 17, 1999, would end up becoming a date forever etched in my soul. Brennen began to go downhill. The doctors and nurses were in and out of his room. He began crashing so hard that my body was trembling all over with fear—it was uncontrollable. I saw a rush of activity enter his room and heard alarms going off. The doctors and nurses began administering CPR again.

We had to get out of their way, so I went into the bathroom in the hallway that was close to his room. It was a single bathroom—it was just me and a mirror, and for the first time in a long time I cried out to God for help. I felt a desperation that I had never known in my life. Tears streaming down my face, I stared into the mirror and heard the Holy Spirit say, "Heather, this is about you coming back to me." It stopped me dead in my tracks. I was stunned. The God I believed in and knew as a little girl was right there with me. He had never left me, even though I was living my life without Him.

I walked out of the bathroom and made it back to the room where Brennen was. Surrounded by both of our parents, the nurses and doctors, and my husband, I held Brennen in my arms as we watched him peacefully slip into eternity with Jesus. There was a peace that surrounded us in that little hospital room. I knew Brennen was no longer with us anymore. I knew Jesus was with us and that He was the peace I felt. I tangibly felt His presence in the darkest moment of my life, but I knew in that moment it was okay to let Brennen go.

After what seemed like a short moment but I'm sure it was much longer, the nurse came in to take Brennen's body. Everything seemed to happen so fast. When we were ready to leave the hospital, I remember walking into the elevator and a nurse who had cared for Brennen was also leaving. As the doors closed, she looked at us and began sobbing. Brennen's death that day had an impact on more than just us. The nurse looked exhausted, and in a strange way her breakdown brought me comfort, knowing that she had cared so much. As my husband drove us home, I laid down the seat in my car and cried the whole way.

As we drove, snow was falling outside, which was not a common occurrence where we lived. After all, El Paso is known as the Sun City because it's mostly always sunny. The rare falling snow stood out to me for many reasons. Even though it was such a cold, dark day, I didn't know at that time, but God was already showing me some beauty in my ashes. Later I learned in the that snow represents purity and repentance. I eventually had the revelation from Jesus that as Brennen died and that season was ending, I was entering into a season of being made new and cleansed by His blood. I was being washed white as snow.

Once home that afternoon, I saw my mom and sister running around the house gathering up Brennen's stuff that was left all over so that I didn't have to see it. But I did see it. I felt it. I could see the black stain on the carpet from the boots worn by the paramedics. I could smell his blanket that had been wrapped around him to keep him warm and comfortable. I could feel the absence of his presence as if a part of me had been ripped off my body. I could feel the sensation of my body telling me it was time to nurse, and there was nothing I could do about it. I could see his bouncer in the kitchen and swing in the living room. I could walk into his room and hear the silence. I could hold his toys but not him. I didn't understand how I could be living this nightmare that only others lived. How was this my story? Where do I go from here? Do I even want to go on from here? I was lost and confused, and the grief was too much to bear.

Have you ever been in a situation where you could see the remnants of something that is no longer there? Like little reminders that you are not crazy, this was actually your life, but now it's gone. The void was tangible. I died inside.

As I lay down on my bed that evening in shock, my husband lying next to me, I had the most amazing, unexpected supernatural experience. I felt this overwhelming energy pass through my body. It was the same feeling that I had experienced as a young girl. The weight of God was back. His fire burning through my body. I could not move or talk as if I were paralyzed—I could only lie there under the weight of it. Like I mentioned before, it wasn't a scary feeling; it felt like God was with me. There was His presence again trying to break through the darkness. I began to see an outline of Brennen. I knew God was showing me that Brennen was with Him and he was all right. God was also letting me know that He was with *me* too. He had my baby, and I wasn't going to walk through this alone. God was encompassing it all. I didn't expect Him to show up like that, yet there He was.

As I woke up each morning to a fresh wave of grief over the next few days, I could feel Jesus compelling me to take His hand—like an invitation to trust Him in this unthinkable situation and an invitation for His presence to be with me. He was like a light showing me a way through the darkness. As I was pulled to be with God and find out who He was and what He was inviting me into, I also found myself in intense grief for the next weeks, months, and years.

I longed to be around Brennen's things. His room, stuffed animals, and tiny clothes—I had to remember this had been real. I needed to be reminded of him and to keep his memory going. Grief came like a hurricane and didn't relent. I would come to find that Jesus's presence was the eye of this storm.

So many people rallied around us during this time—even people we didn't know. The funeral was paid for by family and friends. My mom got herself together and took charge of all the details for the funeral. She even picked out his outfit and mine to wear. I didn't know it at the time, but she had bought two of the same outfit for him—one for him to wear to be buried in and one to give me later as a keepsake of what he wore. I went through the motions. We had many visitors, but I could not bring myself out of my room to see them.

His funeral was held in a little town called Mathis, Texas. This is where my grandma lived at the time. The cemetery there was where my grandfather was buried as well as my grandmother's first baby. She had a son who died shortly after being born. Her son and mine are buried close together. I remember the day of the funeral. I remember a lot of people being there. I remember writing a letter and my sister Holly reading it to everyone in attendance. Not sure how she had the courage to do it, but she did it for me because that's the kind of sister she is. This was a way for me to share my heart without getting up and saying anything, because attending a funeral for your child is too surreal of an experience.

I wish I could say that after the funeral I found closure and never had to struggle again with grief, but that would be lying. Funerals are not closure really; they're just an event to attend that we never asked to be invited to. The two years after Brennen died were hard, to say the least. Everywhere I turned I couldn't escape the fact that Brennen was gone. It was the worst pain I had ever experienced. I found ways to feel guilty, as if it had been my fault. I somehow made it through normal activities like grocery shopping or running errands. In the middle of stores as I watched people just living their normal lives, I remember feeling like I wanted to scream out loud, "Don't you know my son is gone!" Not only was I grieving his physical loss, but there is also a process of grieving all the plans we'd made for our children. The hopes and dreams, the firsts, the "never will I get to see them …"

The memory that plagued me the most was the image of him lying on my living room floor with paramedics all around and seeing him not breathing. It was my constant companion and would play over and over in my mind. I couldn't escape it. I began to suffer with migraines and vertigo. Stress does strange things to our physical bodies. At some point in this journey, I started seeing a therapist. I was not able to handle anything that caused stress. Driving on the freeway about undid me. We moved from El Paso to Austin about three months after he passed. I had to leave. Looking back, I know God had a plan. Our house sold within the first three days of being on the market, and when my husband's boss reached out to a friend of his in Austin, he had a new job just as fast.

It was only when I really grabbed ahold of Jesus's hand and allowed him to enter my pain and suffering that I began to gain footing underneath me. He offered me His peaceful presence. He gave me new glasses to see through the fog of loss and into the realm of truth—His truth. He invited me to experience the Father's heart in all those moments. He never left me but comforted me through it all. After about two years of intense grief, I slowly began to feel freedom from the intense heaviness and grief.

Over time God delivered me completely from the intense grief, hopelessness, and despair. Never to forget, of course, but not having to walk in the bondage of grief or the spirit of heaviness that often comes from loss. God is good like that. He truly wants healing and freedom for us all. All this time I've never taken for granted the way God walked me through that darkness. He is my life. I love His presence and stability of peace in times of turbulence. I love Jesus more than anything in this world and want everyone to experience the freedom I have experienced.

God has continued to walk with me on this crazy ride of life. There are a lot of stories I have with Him, but those are for another time! Cultivating more of Him in my life and Him crafting me over time has led me to discover a deeper meaning to my suffering. I also learned to trust Him more deeply along the way. My heart behind sharing this story is that you will find encouragement amid your trials, tribulations, afflictions, pain, and grief. My hope is that His presence will engulf you and that you will find rest in your hard stories. My prayer is that you will see the difficulties through the lens of Jesus and not just from the natural world.

I want to encourage you that these unexpected stories of pain can have purpose in our lives—fruit will be grown to serve the kingdom of God. How is this possible? Letting Jesus walk you through it. I ask you to let Jesus take your hand and lead you to the other side of fear, trauma, and suffering. Let Him lead you to a place that you could not dream of even if you wanted to. What He does in our lives when we trust Him is beyond our ability to conjure up on our own—it's unthinkable. We live in a fallen world, and we will suffer. But we can suffer to suffer, or we can suffer in Him and come out on the other side with an abundance of gifts that only Jesus can give. Beautiful fruit will grow from our heartache when we invite Him into our circumstances. He blessed me with joy, I was eventually able to say that I am okay with what I went through because I got more of Jesus from it.

My prayer as you read this book is that it gives you hope in Jesus. I know He can do for you what He did for me. Invite Him into your story of pain or sin or whatever you are struggling with and allow Him to change you from the inside out. In the end it's His story and He gets the glory! Without God, my story would just be another tragedy. But because of Him, it's a testimony of His great love. He has a love story for you too. His great redemption and compassion are for me and for you. Philippians 1:29 (NLT) says, "For you have been given not only the privilege of trusting in Christ but also the privilege of suffering for him." See, the story is not wasted. Let's walk this hard season of life you are in together. I want to help you change your perspective to a place of hope and healing, of possibility and purpose, of surrender and repentance. I want you to leave a place of barren destruction and enter a life full of the fruit that only Jesus can grow. He takes the dry, dead aftermath of our suffering and replaces it with healthy, abundant life when we ask Him. Psalm 145:18 tells us, "The LORD is close to all who call on Him, yes, to all who call on Him in truth."

The secret to walking through our hard times is the presence of Jesus with us and in us. The presence of God will radically change your life. It's like this incredible gift that wraps around us, bringing comfort, clarity, power, and strength when life gets tough. Jesus said that it was to our advantage that He went away so He could send the Helper. The helper Jesus sent is Himself living in us. Let that sink in. John 16:5–7 says, "But now I am going to him who sent me. None of you asks me, 'Where are you going?' Rather, you are filled with grief because I have said these things. But very truly I tell you, it is for your good that I am going away. Unless I go away, the Advocate will not come to you; but if I go, I will send him to you." We have the power of God in us as Christ followers, and this is what enables us to live life as an overcomer.

In the book *Don't Miss Out* by Jennie Cunnion, she writes, "I need you to know that whatever lies before you, it's not all on you! It's on the Spirit in you. And if His power can raise our Savior from the grave, He can handle whatever hardship or fear you face."[1] The Holy Spirit in me gave me the power to move forward. The Holy Spirit gave me the comfort I needed each day. He reminded me of God's truth and helped me get free from the enemy's traps.

Right now, you may feel like something in you has died as a result of this unthinkable situation. However, it's the perfect setup for the biggest comeback of your life, but you won't know unless you take Jesus's hand and invite His presence in to transform you. Death is where resurrection begins. It's God's specialty.

How can the worst things in life be made into the best growth of your life? This is known as a paradox. And the answer is Jesus. I'm going to take you on a journey to surrender your pain at the feet of Jesus, to get up out of the grave and grab ahold of His hand. This is where in faith you will trade the pain and loss for a life with Jesus, where you will learn to live in His presence, where your broken mind-set will be renewed by His Word, and you will begin living for a greater purpose than just surviving. Just come as you are. Are you ready to start building an unshakable, firm foundation on Jesus?

Are you stuck wrestling with the question of why this happened to you if God is so good? We all wrestle with this question, so let's spend some time in the next chapter exploring what God has told us in His Word about the condition of the world we live in.

---

[1]   Jennie Cunnion, *Don't Miss Out: Daring to Believe Life Is Better with the Holy Spirit* (Minneapolis, MN: Bethany House, 2021), #25.

Reflection

Hey there, friend, let's have a real heart-to-heart, okay? Think about that painful memory, that tough chapter in your life—we've all got one, or maybe more. Now, if you've never laid that story at Jesus's feet, I really want to encourage you to start doing that. It's a game changer, trust me!

Picture this: you, Jesus, and a cup of coffee, just pouring out your heart. Tell Him exactly how you feel, what you're going through, or what you went through—no holding back. He already knows the deal, but there's something powerful about putting it into words. So, have that conversation with Him.

Now, here's the transforming transaction: invite Him into that painful situation or memory. Tell Him that you want only what He can bring to the table. It's the beginning of taking hold of His hand in faith. As you bring Him into the mix, you're also saying yes to His invitation to turn your ashes into something beautiful.

Let Him know you're trading heartache and loss for His healing, peace, and a sense of purpose arising from the pain. It's like a divine exchange. And here's the reality: Jesus is all about it. He's not just standing by; He wants to dive into the process with you.

So, what do you say? Take a moment, have that conversation with Him, and let's see how He can bring freedom and healing into your story. It's time to let Jesus work His supernatural power in your life. You ready?

CHAPTER 2

The Age-Old Question

"The thief's purpose is to steal and kill and destroy. My purpose is to give them a rich and satisfying life."
~ John 10:10

You might be wondering, "How can someone move from a place of despair or a haunting memory to a place of freedom, purpose, and being close to His presence?" When we are struggling in our pain, we all seem to have this common question on our mind: "How can a loving God allow pain and suffering?" As human beings, we all must face this question at one point or another in our lifetime. We can't escape it, and we can't fully understand it either. However, our Father God, the God who created both you and me, is full of compassion and doesn't leave us empty-handed. To dig a little deeper into this question, let's go back to see how it all began and how the beginning ultimately led us to the cross of Jesus Christ.

Without an understanding of the first book in the Bible, Genesis, i.e., how things began and how we got to where we are, the cross of Jesus won't make much sense. According to *The Hayford Bible Handbook*, "Unless we discern God's original design, created dignity, and intended destiny for humanity at the outset, we will misread His motive and manner in carrying out His plan of redemption. The 'kingdom' key to Genesis is wrapped in the truth that God created humankind as partners, not as peons (i.e., not serfs, drudges, or pawns). While infinitely less than equal with God, humankind was nonetheless created for partnership with Him."[2]

Genesis 1:1 declares, "In the beginning God created the heavens and the earth." God created all things. We are a part of His workmanship. Genesis 1:26–27 says, "Then God said, 'Let us make human beings in our image, to be like us. They will reign over the fish in the sea, the birds in the sky, the livestock, all the wild animals on the earth, and the small animals that scurry along the ground. So God created human beings in his own image. In the image of God he created them; male and female he created them."

So here it all began. God created this amazing world we live in. He created us to rule and subdue it. That's our birthright. To be His children and live in relationship with Him. We were the crown of His creation, so to speak. He gave us free will so that we could make choices, create, experience, and love. Each child would be perfectly thought out with a unique personality and purpose. Psalm 139:14–16 states, "Thank you for making me so wonderfully complex! Your workmanship is marvelous-how well I know it. You watched me as I was being formed in utter seclusion, as I was woven together in the dark of the womb. You saw me before I was born. Every day of my life was recorded in your book. Every moment was laid out before a single day had passed."

God fully knows each of us, and He has invited us to know Him. He gave us His love so we in return could love Him back. This scripture can seem false when we hold it up to the reality of the world we live in. My son, Brennen, was born with a heart defect. He was born sick. That doesn't sound marvelously made, does it?

---

[2]   Jack W. Hayford, ed., *The Hayford Bible Handbook: The Complete Companion for Spirit-Filled Bible Study* (Nashville, TN: Thomas Nelson, 2004), # 2.

How can we make sense of this contradicting reality—the world we live in versus the one that these scriptures are describing? In Genesis, we learn how creation began, but we also learn how things fell apart. Why is the world that we live in fallen? Why do we feel so far from God? Why do we feel so broken? Why do bad things happen in the world we live in? How can God help me anyway? There are many questions we can ask ourselves to try to make sense of this world.

Tucked away in Genesis 3 is a lesson about why we live in a fallen state. When God created Adam and Eve, He put them in a place called the garden of Eden. There was a tree in this garden that God had prohibited Adam and Eve to eat from. Genesis 2:15–17 says, "The LORD God placed the man in the garden of Eden to tend and watch over it. But the Lord God warned him, 'You may freely eat the fruit of every tree in the garden-except the tree of the knowledge of good and evil. If you eat its fruit, you are sure to die.'"

We next find Eve being tempted by the serpent to eat from this forbidden tree. The serpent twists God's words and tries to get her to choose to eat from this tree. Genesis 3:1(NLT) tells us that, "The serpent was the shrewdest of all the wild animals the Lord God had made. One day he asked the woman, 'Did God really say you must not eat the fruit from any of the trees in the garden?'" Eve goes on to tell the serpent that she is allowed to eat from the trees, it's only the tree in the middle of the garden that they can't eat. Genesis 3:4–6 (NLT) continues, "'You won't die!' the serpent replied to the woman. 'God knows that your eyes will be opened as soon as you eat it, and you will be like God, knowing both good and evil.' The woman was convinced. She saw that the tree was beautiful and its fruit looked delicious, and she wanted the wisdom it would give her. So she took some of the fruit and ate it. Then she gave some to her husband, who was with her, and he ate it, too."

In the next part of the story God calls out to Adam and Eve; they were hiding in the trees because their eyes were now open and they knew they were naked. God asked them how they knew this and if they had eaten from the tree they were not supposed to have eaten from.

We were never meant to grow old and die or get sick; why do you think we fight it so much? We were created to live in relationship with God forever. I've often heard people ask, why did God create that tree in the garden in the first place? I believe that the garden of Eden was so closely entwined with God's presence and that's why the tree of knowledge and tree of life were located there. Adam and Eve were living with God's presence; He walked with them. He gave them free will because that was the only way for them to truly love Him back.

When God enters the garden after the fall, He institutes the consequences for Adam and Eve's actions. They would no longer live in the garden of Eden. They would be sent out and the presence of God would no longer walk with them. His presence left, and sin entered the world. Physical death became the wages of sin. As Romans 6:23 says, "For the wages of sin is death, but the free gift of God is eternal life through Christ Jesus our Lord." All of creation would feel the effects of sin.

God drove them out of Eden. By His grace He kept them from eating from the tree of life in their sin state. Can you imagine if they had eaten from the tree of life, and we all had to live forever in our fallen mess? No, thank you! Genesis 3:22–23 (NLT) says, "Then the Lord God said, 'Look, the human beings have become like us, knowing both good and evil. What if they reach out, take fruit from the tree of life, and eat it? Then they will live forever!' So the Lord God banished them from the garden of Eden, and he sent Adam out to cultivate the ground from which he had been made." Mercy was already at play. There were many trees in the garden they could eat from—there was only one forbidden tree. God never told them not to eat from the tree of life—only from the tree of knowledge of good and evil. It was only after they disobeyed and ate from the forbidden tree of knowledge that God became concerned that they would eat from the tree of life and live forever in their state of sin.

When sin entered the world, it set the stage for things to come. Mankind lost God's presence. We became far from God, our Creator. As a result, relationships between husbands and their wives became harder. Divorce became a thing. Our physical bodies experienced sickness. Weather patterns became destructive. Accidents became unavoidable. Our minds, emotions, and wills became selfish. We started to experience jealousy, rage, and anger. Hatred, rape, human trafficking, pornography, slavery, racism, and murder followed. Addictions of all kinds perpetuated. Our mental health declined. Gender and sexual orientation became twisted. Suicide entered the minds of people. Hunger and need spread all over the world. The list goes on and on. But to top it off, death entered the world. Everything has been touched by sin.

The worst part, however, was the separation from the sustaining presence of God. Sin is described in the Bible as the transgression of the law of God. Mankind rebelled against Him. Romans 5:12 states, "When Adam sinned, sin entered the world. Adam's sin brought death, so death spread to everyone, for everyone sinned." Nothing has escaped death. People die. Some kids get sick. Some babies never grow up. Any and everything has been the result of that first sin being ushered into the world.

Doesn't seem very promising, does it? So here we are left to chance, it seems. Where is God? Did He leave us because of our disobedience, never to be seen again? Is all lost? Are we born just to die and go from one hard experience to another? We may feel burdened with a lot of questions as to where we go from here. Life can feel a bit overwhelming and hopeless in this state. In fact, at some point, we all suffer from the effects of sin and must come to terms with it in our world and in ourselves.

So where do we go from here? If we want to live a life of purpose, freedom, and healing, then we must run to our Savior Jesus—into His comfort and care. In this place His presence never leaves us but instead sustains us and redeems us. It's His presence that brings us comfort, peace, direction, and healing when we experience painful things.

I remember a few months after my son died, we would visit my grandmother every month. My husband would drive us the long drive, three-and-a-half-hours to see Mam-ma, as we fondly called her, in a little town called Mathis, Texas, so I could visit Brennen at the cemetery where he was buried. She would make us a lovely meal each time. Her specialty was a roast, and I can still smell it in my memory to this day. I learned a lot of her recipes and believe I can cook like her, too—well, that's what my family tells me anyway. She loved to laugh and tell stories; it was comforting to be in her presence. We were kindred spirits, she and I, both not having to say a word about what had happened to us but knowing the "club" we both belonged to. Although I could only be in her comforting presence once a month, Jesus's presence is always there. His comfort never leaves us. He promises us this in scripture. Deuteronomy 31:6 says, "So be strong and courageous! Do not be afraid and do not panic before them. For the Lord your God will personally go ahead of you. He will neither fail you nor abandon you." It doesn't matter what the world can take from us—if we have Jesus, we have everything!

It would seem that all hope was lost after what happened in the garden of Eden. Mankind was destined to die, subject to traumatic events, trials, and tribulations around every corner. But God. While we were still sinners, He had a plan for His children—to restore all that was lost. John 3:16 says, "For this is how God loved the world:

He gave his one and only Son, so that everyone who believes in him will not perish but have eternal life."

You can't talk about God without talking about Jesus Christ. Jesus was and is God's plan for restoration. The Bible tells us the history of God's people and what He wants us to know about Him. It describes His love for us and His plan to restore all that was lost. Jesus is our way back into right relationship with God. Jesus is Immanuel, God with us. Jesus is the Word made flesh. Jesus is the sacrificial lamb who was slain for all mankind. It is by faith in Jesus that we are saved, not by works so that no one can boast. Ephesians 2:8 states "For it is by grace you have been saved, through faith—and this is not from yourselves, it is the gift of God." We cannot earn our salvation. This is the gospel message. This is the good news of Jesus Christ. In Revelation 22:1–5 the tree of life is mentioned again. This is a picture of restoration:

> Then the angel showed me the river of the water of life, as clear as crystal, flowing from the throne of God and of the Lamb down the middle of the great street of the city. On each side of the river stood the tree of life, bearing twelve crops of fruit, yielding its fruit every month. And the leaves of the tree are for the healing of the nations. No longer will there be any curse. The throne of God and of the Lamb will be in the city, and his servants will serve him. They will see his face, and his name will be on their foreheads. There will be no more night. They will not need the light of a lamp or the light of the sun, for the Lord God will give them light. And they will reign for ever and ever.

God is restoring us back to Him through Jesus, and it starts the minute we take His hand. We know why sin entered the world and why there is so much heartache. On the other side of the story, we have this hope in Jesus Christ. So, if Jesus came to set things back in right order, why is there still so much drama in this life? We are in the middle of God's story. We are living in the time where the enemy is still prowling around. But Jesus's sacrifice on the cross defeated the enemy by taking away Satan's power to hold sinners to the debt of their sins and trespasses. We are now free to grapple against the spiritual forces of evil and Satan's schemes, knowing we will get the victory. Make no mistake, death was defeated on the cross. Death is not our final destiny. Jesus will come again and make things right. We are waiting for His return. But in the meantime, we each have a decision to make. Will we accept this gift from God to be back in His presence, or will we continue down our own path?

We have free will to choose either option. In the end, though, one path leads to eternal life and the other, eternal separation from Father God. When we accept this gift of salvation, we become a new creation. We are born again. God places the Holy Spirit in us. Think about it: God is in us! It's like having a supernatural secret weapon.

With His presence in us, He truly will never leave or forsake us. With His presence in us, we now have the power to live as overcomers of anything that is thrown our way. As we enter a relationship with our Father God through Jesus's sacrifice, our minds are renewed, and we begin to see things from a new perspective. We start to see God's truth. We realize the love that God has for us is beyond our comprehension. We are His children, and He wishes none of us to perish. He provided a way back to Him—if we want it. Once we enter this relationship, we begin to live for Him because we see our sin and His sacrifice more clearly.

How do we live in the space between the cross and eternal life? We seek to know Him more, and we remember the enemy has been defeated. Things still happen that are tragic and unjust. Jesus has not set up the new heaven and earth yet. Part of being a disciple of Jesus is learning to navigate this space, this tension. I often catch myself thinking, "If only this piece of the puzzle were fixed or removed or changed, then my life would be perfect." I have even tried to assure God that if He would remove a particular problem, then "I promise" I'd serve Him. He has assured me it doesn't work like that. I have to serve Him and trust Him despite my circumstances. I have to surrender the "even if" and the "even though" thoughts. This is faith, everyone. This is trusting Jesus with everything we have.

When Brennen passed away, it felt like everything I ever knew and trusted was gone in an instant. I realized I had zero control in this world. Have you had your sense of control ripped away by something? It's a scary realization to be confronted with the fact that we are not in control. This is how we know that everything we've built on our own is sinking sand; it's unstable and can be gone in an instant. There is only one way to stand steady and firm in this world. That is on the firm foundation of Jesus Christ. Matthew 7:24–27 assures us of this:

> Therefore everyone who hears these words of mine and puts them into practice is like a wise man who built his house on the rock. The rain came down, the streams rose, and the winds blew and beat against that house; yet it did not fall, because it had its foundation on the rock. But everyone who hears these words of mine and does not put them into practice is like a foolish man who built his house on sand. The rain came down, the streams rose, and the winds blew and beat against that house, and it fell with a great crash.

Trusting Jesus is a journey. It can be especially difficult when we feel so much pain and hurt. We don't know if we can trust Him. It takes time to surrender the hurt and pain to Him and to see how He will work in our lives. It can be day by day and sometimes even moment by moment. For our sake, He is patient and gentle. For me, I knew that if I didn't trust Him, I wouldn't make it.

And guess what? We are not alone! As we read through the scriptures, we find countless stories of men and women who suffered and walked with God through their suffering. There is so much encouragement in these stories for us to glean from. It's incredible how, amid all that hardship, they didn't let suffering break them. Take David, the shepherd king, for example; his Psalms are full of painful trials. But he held on tight to the promises of God, and in return, he found a sanctuary for his sorrow during everything he walked through. Then there's Moses who led the Israelites through one thing after another in the wilderness. His talks with God up Mount Sinai became his compass, offering guidance and assurance. And Ruth, navigating the loss of her family and her displacement, found redemption and restoration by embracing the God of Israel. These aren't just ancient tales; they are mirror images reflecting our own struggles today. They show us that even in the toughest times, knowing God intimately will be our anchor, giving us strength and lasting hope. These stories are timeless reminders of how faith transforms us and how embracing God in our suffering brings light in the dark.

Do you feel like you are in a situation where you might not make it? Or have you not recovered from something in the past? Are you hoping for a lifeline to pull you up and out of what you are or have been stuck in? As you have read above, I understand the desperation of needing relief from the pain. Here's the thing. There is no easy fix this side of heaven. There's not a perfect 1, 2, 3 and A, B, C to-do list. We want it to be easy, and we desperately want control because we've lost all sense of control and what seemed to be a firm foundation. The only way to be healed is through the supernatural presence of Jesus Christ. It's nothing we can do on our own.

Walking out of the web of heartache and pain is never simple. We must learn a new way of living. A new way of thinking. A new way of surrendering and trusting in a holy God. The only path to true freedom, purpose, and healing in this journey is Jesus. He alone has the power to set us free, heal our wounds, and give us abundant lives despite it all.

I hope you begin to feel a glimmer of hope for yourself and your story. Jesus, after all, is the hope for all mankind. It's in His presence that you will begin to see your story change. Jesus knows you well, but He is calling you back to a place where you know Him well too. He has invited you into something amazing; the question is, will you invite Him in as well? Will you grab ahold of His hand and allow Him to change your mind-set and teach you how to live in His presence so that you can live a life of purpose? This will take a stance of humility on your part, but this is the perfect place to receive all God has for you.

As we reflect on God's story of creation and how we got to where we are, we find a common thread that binds us all: the transformative power of God's presence. From the beginning of our existence, God designed us for partnership and intimate relationship with Him. The consequences of the fall, vividly portrayed in Genesis, led to a world tainted by sin and suffering. Yet the overarching narrative unveils a divine plan of redemption through Jesus Christ, restoring what was lost. We learned that the timeless stories of David, Moses, and Ruth resonate as testimonies of individuals who, amid suffering, intimately knew and embraced God to find peace, purpose, and healing in His unwavering presence. As we live between the cross and eternal life, the invitation is clear: embrace the transformative journey, grab ahold of His hand, and step into the profound relationship our Father calls us into.

In the next chapter, we will explore the depths of our Father's heart for each of us and discover what Jesus is inviting us into when we take His hand and enter this transformative journey.

Reflection

Picture this: you and me sitting down, sipping on some coffee, having a heart-to-heart. You know, if you've never had that heart-to-heart with Jesus, inviting Him to be the Lord and Savior of your life, I'd really encourage you to start there. It's a game changer.

And hey, if you've ever felt like you've veered off the path a bit, no worries. The beautiful thing is you can always hit the reset button. It's like a fresh start, a do-over. The Bible says, "You will seek me and find me when you seek me with all your heart" (Jeremiah 29:13). Trust me, that's a promise you can count on.

Now, here's the real deal: to see Jesus, our spirits need a rebirth. It's like a transformation from the inside out. Check out John 3:1–21. We've got to face the truth: we're all sinners in need of a Savior.

So, whether you've just embraced Jesus as your Savior or been on this journey for a while, it's a good moment to reflect on your relationship with Him. Are you in deep, committed companionship, or is it more of a fair-weather friendship?

We all come to this crossroads in our faith where we've got to decide—are we all-in or are we out? There's no middle ground. Jesus is not just our Savior; He's the Lord of our lives. When we surrender, have faith, and walk in humility with Him, that's when the real magic of a relationship with Jesus unfolds. It's not just a label; it's a living, breathing connection. So, what do you say we go all-in together?

CHAPTER 3

Jesus Is Inviting Us to Know the Father's Heart

"God never said that the journey would be easy, but He did say that the arrival would be worthwhile."
~ Max Lucado

Whatever story brought you to this painful place is not your final chapter. If we don't grasp that Jesus is inviting us into something more than what has happened to us, then we have the tendency to allow it to define us. Our goal is to be defined by God and not our circumstances. We might not have all the answers this side of eternity, but as we discussed in the last chapter, we do have a good understanding of why bad things happen in this world. Therefore, it's imperative that we understand the Father's heart in order to process our pain with Him. Our perception of God can be tainted due to lack of knowledge of Scripture or to the actions of other people.

We have all felt the despair of something that was sacred to us be torn from our lives. Maybe it was a marriage, the loss of a loved one, as in my case, or a dream you worked so hard to achieve only to see it crumble. The core meaning of *sacred* is to be connected to God or something that brings awe and respect. What if we need to change our perspective to Jesus's perspective of what happened, to link our suffering to the sacredness of God, so we can be connected to the one who created us? When we let God mold and shape our heartache, we will begin to see it as a sacred place that Jesus healed us in. We will begin to see His heart for us, and our perspective will change.

If you have ever heard the song "Held" sung by Natalie Grant and written by Christa Nichole Wells, then you will understand the emotion that it brings when played on the radio. This song is about a two-month-old baby boy who passed away and perfectly describes how I felt. Every time I hear this song, time stops for a moment, and I go back to that place when Brennen passed away. Is there a song, a place, or a person who takes you back to your moment of heartbreak? When these moments happen, allow yourself to go back to how it all felt. You know why? So that you can remember. I don't ever want to forget what God has done in me through this story. We are held by the hands of God in our darkest moments.

If you have experienced the loss of a child or someone close to you, I want to say how sorry I am. At some point we all face loss in one way or another. Loss is a universal language that we don't sign up for willingly, yet it forces our hand eventually. There are so many things that can bring about loss, suffering, and grief in our lives. We think it will only happen to others, but none of us are exempt.

Years before Brennen was ever born, I watched a woman on a talk show share about the loss of her child. As I folded laundry on my living room couch, I remember thinking, "I cannot fathom going through something like that." I told myself that only happens to others. Not long after that, I found myself in the same story, the one I said I could not survive. The one I could not fathom. Yet here I was in someone else's nightmare; only, it was mine. We truly cannot imagine how things feel to someone going through it unless we, too, have experienced the same loss. I did not have God's presence or perspective at that point in my life. I didn't know Him; I only knew about Him.

One of the things that I learned about Jesus is that He wants to enter our pain and suffering with us, and while He holds us through it, we experience His supernatural peace and presence. We begin to truly see His heart for us.

As the days went by after Brennen's death, I began finding ways to keep myself busy. I worked on a scrapbook of pictures and things that reminded me of him. I wanted to feel Brennen's presence, so I found ways to mimic it—by finding and doing things that kept his memory alive. My whole family bought matching necklaces to wear every day as a reminder of him. In fact, to this day my husband has never stopped wearing his. We started lighting a special candle on Sundays in honor of his memory.

I started pouring myself into reading the Bible for the first time in my life. I began craving God's Word and praying to Him. My soul needed a place to process the loss and to cry out and release it, because keeping it all in felt like I would suffocate. This is what kept me going, and a new awareness of His presence developed in me. I wasn't alone in my pain. Jesus became my connection to Brennen. He was inviting me to fill the void with His presence—something that would never leave me. Something I could count on no matter what.

In Second Samuel 12 there is a story about King David and the loss of his infant son. There was one line I became attached to. It compelled me to stay close to Jesus. David was essentially mourning for his child while he was still alive, but after the baby died, he got up and went about his business. His servants asked him why, and he said, "But why should I fast when he is dead? Can I bring him back again? I will go to him one day, but he cannot return to me." (2 Samuel 12:23 NLT). I had that same realization that I could go to Brennen one day, but also, I would get to be with Jesus in heaven. I knew my heart needed Jesus for this. I knew I wouldn't survive this grief if I didn't remain close to His presence. This compelled me to run to the arms of Jesus. I hope that you are beginning to see God's love for you. That He longs to be with us through every experience we go through.

About a week after Brennen died, my husband and I met with our friend's pastor at their church. At this point my husband, who never went to church growing up or even knew who God was, just followed me right along on this journey. Which is a miracle itself. The pastor sat with us and heard our story and prayed with us to accept Jesus Christ as our Lord and Savior. It still amazes me to this day that God revealed Himself so clearly to us and no one had to say a word. God's presence was so powerful, we just ran straight into His arms, and He held us. We both can vividly remember walking out of that pastor's office and feeling like we had been changed. We had been born again within a week of Brennen's passing and could feel that we were each a new creation.

Through the death of our son, in our town with the nickname Sun City, we found life in the Son, Jesus Christ. We could feel His presence, and in return we began to experience hope, peace, and purpose. We were experiencing His love for us. We began going to church and gathering with Christians because we needed to know everything we could about God and His Word. We were tasting and seeing that God is good, and we couldn't get enough! We were beginning to see a glimpse of God's heart for us and what Jesus was inviting us into.

God wants to prosper us, give us a hope, a future, and not harm us. He wants us to trade a life of bondage for a life of freedom and healing. This is the Father's heart! We can be in bondage to fear, emotional turmoil, abuse, trauma, grief, and distorted ways of thinking. He is a good Father, and if we don't understand His love for us, then we can get lost in the fog of pain.

The Father's heart was also displayed on the cross. God's Word says He is close to the brokenhearted. This means He is near when we experience hurt and pain. He wants us to surrender it all and confess we can't do it on our own, we can't keep going in the direction we are headed, but also that we don't know how to move from the place we are in. It's in this posture of surrender that we realize how desperate we are for a Savior. Jesus longs to hold us and bring us healing. He does not leave us stranded on the side of the highway of pain. I'm challenging your current perspective to see the benefit of processing your pain in Jesus. To walk this process in His presence.

Did you know that Jesus was well acquainted with pain and suffering too? Since He also experienced it, He is more than able to get us through it. Let's look at Isaiah 53 and imagine how Jesus was treated, the pain He endured, and the suffering He went through, so that we know, Jesus truly knows pain and suffering. Isaiah 53:1–12 reads,

> Who has believed our message and to whom has the arm of the LORD been revealed? He grew up before him like a tender shoot, and like a root out of dry ground. He had no beauty or majesty to attract us to him, nothing in his appearance that we should desire him. He was despised and rejected by mankind, a man of suffering, and familiar with pain. Like one from whom people hide their faces he was despised, and we held him in low esteem. Surely he took up our pain and bore our suffering, yet we considered him punished by God, stricken by him, and afflicted. But he was pierced for our transgressions, he was crushed for our iniquities; the punishment that brought us peace was on him, and by his wounds we are healed. We all, like sheep, have gone astray, each of us has turned to our own

way; and the LORD has laid on him the iniquity of us all. He was oppressed and afflicted, yet he did not open his mouth; he was led like a lamb to the slaughter, and as a sheep before its shearers is silent, so he did not open his mouth. By oppression and judgment he was taken away. Yet who of his generation protested? For he was cut off from the land of the living; for the transgression of my people he was punished. He was assigned a grave with the wicked, and with the rich in his death, though he had done no violence, nor was any deceit in his mouth. Yet it was the LORD's will to crush him and cause him to suffer, and though the LORD makes his life an offering for sin, he will see his offspring and prolong his days, and the will of the LORD will prosper in his hand. After he has suffered, he will see the light of life and be satisfied; by his knowledge my righteous servant will justify many, and he will bear their iniquities. Therefore I will give him a portion among the great, and he will divide the spoils with the strong, because he poured out his life unto death, and was numbered with the transgressors. For he bore the sin of many, and made intercession for the transgressors.

There is no one who has suffered more than Jesus. Not only did He suffer unimaginable physical pain, but He also bore the weight of mankind's sin! He died a horrible death for you and me. Moved by His love for us and desire to see us set free, He went to the cross. We can't even comprehend that. If we are going to identify with and be made like Jesus, then surely God will work through our pain and suffering too. And like Jesus, we have an opportunity to be "resurrected" as well. It's important that we have this paradigm shift in our way of thinking. God is using what we experience here on earth—the ashes—for the benefit of our resurrection—being born again, healed, etc. Our character becomes more Christlike, and our minds renew when we fill it with His living and active Word. All of this bathed in prayer and lived out with His presence brings us to a greater purpose than just heartache and loss—this is what the Father's heart longs for.

First Peter 2:19–25 says,

> For it is commendable if someone bears up under the pain of unjust suffering because they are conscious of God. But how is it to your credit if you receive a beating for doing wrong and endure it? But if you suffer for doing good and you endure it, this is commendable before God. To this you were called, because Christ suffered for you, leaving you an example, that you should follow in his steps. "He committed no sin, and no deceit was found in his mouth." When they hurled their insults at him, he did not retaliate; when he suffered, he made no threats. Instead, he entrusted himself to him who judges justly. He himself bore our sins in his body on the cross, so that we might die to sins and live for righteousness; by his wounds you have been healed. For you were like sheep going astray, but now you have returned to the Shepherd and Overseer of your souls.

Again, we see that Jesus suffered for the will of God to be done. For something better than this life for us. For the glory of God to be seen and felt among us. We, too, are invited into this process. Our suffering can be used to bring about God's purposes and plans—a place where others can see the presence of God at work.

"God is love" according to 1 John 4:8. It's God's heart for us to be healed from the world's definition of love and learn to define love by who He is. He wants us to know *His* love and be healed by *His* love. He comforts us and wraps us in this love and gives us hope so that we can go on. Because of God's love for us He never leaves us or forsakes us. He is a constant companion in our suffering.

Suffering causes us to dig deep and make a choice. Many will ask the question of whether God is even real, while for others who already know God, suffering grows their faith and deepens their trust in Him. They go from head knowledge about God to knowing Him in mind, body, soul, and spirt. This is what endurance produces in us. Hebrews 4:15–16 tells us, "For we do not have a high priest who is unable to empathize with our weaknesses, but we have one who has been tempted in every way, just as we are—yet he did not sin."

Make no mistake: Jesus was fully God but also became fully human. This allowed Him to be with us so we could relate to Him. Because of His experience as fully human, He felt loss, grief, pain, sadness, loneliness, and fear. He felt what we feel. Therefore, He has compassion and empathy for us. Jesus dying on the cross was a perfectly designed plan by a perfect Father. The only way to atone for our sins was for Jesus to come to the earth and offer Himself as the perfect sacrifice. If you're a parent, wouldn't you do anything to rescue your child if they were lost? Well, that is how God feels for all of His creation—all His children ever created. He went to great lengths to make a way for us to come back to Him.

There is only one way to God—Jesus Christ. Some people struggle with this, but I find great comfort in it. God made it clear:

freely accept the gift or don't, it's up to you. His gift can't be earned or bought. It's an invitation for all. It seems simple really. The hard part is we don't want to give up our ways and selfish desires to accept the gift. John 14:6 says, "Jesus answered, 'I am the way, the truth, and the life. No one comes to the Father except through me.'" In John 10:9–10 (NLT) Jesus says, "Yes, I am the gate. Those who come in through me will be saved. They will come and go freely and will find good pastures. The thief's purpose is to steal and kill and destroy. My purpose is to give them a rich and satisfying life." Over and over in the scriptures Jesus makes it clear, He is the way to the Father. He is the door, the gate, and the way. We enter through Him. This is done by faith and receiving what God did for us. It's about acknowledging our need for a Savior because we are sinners and lost. We share in the suffering of Jesus. He suffered but rose again—we, too, suffer and will die, but we will rise again. We have this hope.

So, as we invite Jesus into our pain, we simultaneously accept His invitation into finding purpose. Our suffering, pain, and affliction have eternal purposes. We don't just accept the invitation of Jesus for our salvation, then never think about Him again. We accept the invitation in every aspect of our lives so that He can produce something amazing from His redemption plan in us. Our suffering in Jesus allows us to share in the hope of Jesus.

Romans 8:28 says that "And we know that God causes everything to work together for the good of those who love God and are called according to his purpose for them." First Peter 1:3–6 tells us, "Praise be to God and Father of our Lord Jesus Christ! In his great mercy he has given us new birth into a living hope through the resurrection of Jesus Christ from the dead, and into an inheritance that can never perish, spoil, or fade. This inheritance is kept in heaven for you, who through faith are shielded by God's power until the coming of the salvation that is ready to be revealed in the last time. In all this you greatly rejoice, through now for a little while you may have had to suffer grief of all kinds of trials."

I don't know how people make it through loss or tragedy without Jesus. I think it's impossible. Sure, we can find ways to numb ourselves or entertain ourselves to help us forget, but true healing never takes hold. Fruit isn't grown this way. Jesus is our healer, and He doesn't leave us in our suffering. He walks us through to the other side—healed and whole in Him. He has a way of taking the worst situation and creating something good out of it—healing, new vision, character growth, wisdom, revelation, strength, and compassion for others, to name a few. He holds us together as we are falling apart. He holds our pain in His hands, so we don't have to carry the burden of it. He takes our broken pieces and creates a beautiful mosaic masterpiece, held together by His love.

Maybe you don't want to invite Jesus into the pain, the loss, the trial, or the affliction. Maybe you feel it's just too hard. Maybe in your grief, like I did, you feel guilty for trying to move forward. I remember feeling like if I moved forward, I would forget Brennen, or it would mean I didn't care. It's a horrible thing to feel, a heavy burden to carry.

But Jesus says, "Come to me, all you who are weary and burdened, and I will give you rest. Take my yoke upon you and learn from me, for I am gentle and humble in heart, and you will find rest for your souls. For my yoke is easy and my burden is light" (Matthew 11:28–30). He is the great burden carrier. He doesn't cause us to forget what we went through. In Luke 22:31–32, we read, "Simon, Simon, Satan has asked to sift all of you as wheat. But I have prayed for you, Simon, that your faith may not fail. And when you have turned back, strengthen your brothers." This is an amazing verse with so much revelation to help us. Jesus warned Simon that Satan asked to sift him. This tells me Satan can only go so far; he has boundaries. Only God knows the bigger picture, and He sees the fruit that comes springing forth from our heartache. Jesus then says He is praying for Simon's faith to remain. How amazing is that! Jesus prays for us! After Simon turns back, he is charged with a job: to strengthen his brothers. This is one of the biggest ways God works in our pain. This is our mandate from Jesus when we go through hard times. Jesus's love empowers us to move forward, one step at a time, and then strengthen others with our testimonies!

God exchanges our hopelessness for life, our bondage for freedom, our story of loss for a story of hope and purpose. He supernaturally changes us for the better, so much so that we can even be okay with what we walked through because we have Jesus now. He remains close like a shoulder we can lean on and a shelter we can abide in.

Other paths may help temporarily, but I imagine they are like putting a Band-Aid on a wound to cover it, but it will never fully heal. It will create a numbing experience that lasts but a moment; however, there is no freedom in that. But God wants to turn our pain into ministry. There is nothing better than helping others walk through something we found freedom in through Christ. This is being His hands and feet, and it leads to true freedom. This is another description of God's heart for us—an exchange of our pain for His healing—and then in return, we help others.

Years after I had been walking with the Lord, I remember once telling someone my story. I shared about how much I loved Jesus and all He had walked me through. I remember blurting out that I wouldn't trade what I had walked through for anything because of what I had gained in Christ. My friend shared with me later that she thought that was a crazy thing to say. It was only after entering into her own relationship with Jesus that she could begin to see what I meant. Trust me, I'm not saying I was happy my son died. It's just that the Lord had moved so mightily through this story that I could wholeheartedly see Him and trust Him.

Jesus's love and mercy is more than anything we can walk through on earth. His love is greater than our understanding. I knew His great love for me was real. I knew that He was healing me from the pain of my loss. I knew He was the truth—the highest form of reality. I knew that He entered my pain and suffering with me and that I was not alone. He planted my feet firmly in Him. I gained His presence in me, and I wasn't going to let that go. My loss was what brought me to this truth and understanding of God. God wants to be known. He wants to reveal His Father's heart to us. He wanted me to find His great love and how to abide in Him. And He wants the same for you.

A good father wants the best for his children. He wants his children to feel protected, cared for, seen, loved, provided for; he wants them to know he will carry their burdens that are too heavy. God is this good Father. He is motivated by love because that is His nature—God is love. We can't truly know what love is until we experience it in Him. We get glimmers of love in how our family feels about us and how we feel for our children. But pure love is to really know God and how He loves us. I love how the following scripture speaks of His love and how He longs to reveal His nature to us:

> Dear friends, let us love one another, for love comes from God. Everyone who loves has been born of God and knows God. Whoever does not love does not know God, because God is love. This is how God showed his love among us: He sent his one and only Son into the world that we might live through him. This is love: not that we loved God, but that he loved us and sent his Son as an atoning sacrifice for our sins. Dear friends, since God so loved us, we also ought to love one another. No one has ever seen God; but if we

love one another, God lives in us and his love is made complete in us.

This is how we know that we live in him and he in us: He has given us of his Spirit. And we have seen and testify that the Father has sent his Son to be the Savior of the world. If anyone acknowledges that Jesus is the Son of God, God lives in them and they in God. And so we know and rely on the love God has for us.

God is love. Whoever lives in love lives in God, and God in them. This is how love is made complete among us so that we will have confidence on the day of judgment: In this world we are like Jesus. There is no fear in love. But perfect love drives out fear, because fear has to do with punishment. The one who fears is not made perfect in love.

We love because he first loved us. Whoever claims to love God yet hates a brother or sister is a liar. For whoever does not love their brother and sister, whom they have seen, cannot love God, whom they have not seen. And he has given us this command: Anyone who loves God must also love their brother and sister. (1 John 4:7–21)

This verse teaches us that God is love—not that He *can* love but that His very essence *is* love. One of my favorite verses is "For I am convinced that neither death nor life, neither angels nor demons, neither the present nor the future, nor any powers, neither height nor depth, nor anything else in all creation, will be able to separate us from the love of God that is in Christ Jesus our Lord" (Romans

8:38–39). Read that again and let it sink in. Nothing, absolutely nothing, can separate God's love from us. Not even our sin. He demonstrated His love so deeply for us on the cross. He wasn't willing to lose His children.

God made a way back to Him if we will only have Him. He makes it clear to us in His Word that He will use whatever it takes to get our attention and that nothing can separate His love from us. His word is a revelation of His heart toward us. His love is beyond our understanding. I can think of only one thing keeping us from experiencing this—that is our failure to receive what He freely gave us, through the work of the cross.

We can be our own worst enemy—often stubborn and rebellious. We can easily decide to get angry with God when we experience pain. We tell ourselves, if God was real, then this wouldn't have happened. Or we get bitter. But remember, we don't have to suffer just to suffer if we include God. He takes the circumstances we walk through and brings something beautiful out of them.

It's often in the depths of losing everything that we finally turn to Him. When we hit rock bottom or when the pain becomes too overwhelming, we reach the end of ourselves and cry out "God, if you're there, if you're real, I need you because I'm not going to make it without you!" This moment has the power to alter the trajectory of our entire life for all eternity. Sometimes, the enemy thinks we are done for, but God knows that in navigating through these circumstances, we will come to recognize our desperate need for Him. Remember the arrow analogy? We want Jesus to be the archer, not our circumstance. Only Jesus can course correct the trajectory of our path or mend the broken arrow and make it stronger.

God is the only one who can see the bigger picture in its entirety. But He does give us glimpses. It was God's love that allowed me to see Brennen in a dream. I've always had vivid, colorful dreams my whole life, but after Brennen died, I stopped dreaming. Finally, after about a year and a half, I had the most beautiful dream. When I woke up, I felt the Holy Spirit confirming in me that I hadn't dreamed in a long time because He wanted to give me this dream. He wanted it to stand out and for me to know it was from Him.

In the dream, I was brought into a room and a person who looked like a nurse came in, and she was carrying Brennen. There was no talking—no questions to be asked—we were silent. She handed me Brennen; he was still a baby and wrapped in a blanket. His body seemed to sparkle, and his blue eyes were bluer than I remembered. He looked happy, healthy, and vibrant. He glistened. I knew in my spirit that he had been with Jesus. He was okay, and I could feel peace. Yes, I was sad that I couldn't be with him, but I had peace to let it be. I knew I would be with him again one day, but for now I could rest in Jesus.

From that moment on everything changed for me. I was no longer experiencing intense grief. Jesus had led me through to the other side. He walked with me through the process of loss and changed my perception by His Word and called me into something greater than I had ever imagined. I believe I was radically healed. My spirit was born again through this process of coming back to Jesus and surrendering myself to Him. My emotions were at peace. The physical aches, migraines, and vertigo were gone. All along, the Father's love reigned and brought rest to my weary body and soul, which is His heart for all His children.

I want to introduce you to a woman named Elizabeth Elliot. She was a missionary who lived from 1926 to 2015. Her call cost her dearly in her lifetime. She lost her first husband on the mission field in Ecuador. The very people they came to serve took his life. Elizabeth later returned to this place to minister to the people who took her husband's life. Wow, only God! I love this quote I found online from her that was born out of her suffering and her invitation to grab ahold of God's hand: "The deepest things that I have learned in my own life have come from the deepest suffering. And out of the deepest water and the hottest fires have come the deepest things I know about God." She then went on to say, "Sometimes life is so hard you can only do the next thing. Whatever that is, just do the next thing. God will meet you there." I wholeheartedly agree with her.

As we close this chapter, let's end by considering all that Jesus invites us into and holds for us. Taking a step forward in letting go of your heartache and accepting the invitation to take ahold of Jesus's hand is called surrender. You might be curious how to muster up the strength to reach out. Make no mistake: we can't do this in our own power. There is, however, a supernatural strength just waiting to engulf us.

Reflection

You know the scripture that says "God is love," right? It's a pretty mind-blowing concept. We've grown up in a world that's far from perfect, and our experiences with love might not have been all sunshine and rainbows. Some of us have faced harshness and not-so-loving actions from others, making it a bit tricky to believe in God's unconditional love. But here's the amazing part: when we invite God into our lives and start learning His ways, we get to experience a different kind of love. It's like the love of a Father who's always got our back, never giving up on us.

So, why not ask Him to help you really feel that love, to heal the way you see love and to let you see it through His lens? Let Him guide you out of the pain and wrap you up in His incredible love. Ask God to change your perspective of Him and to see His heart for you. You can pour out your soul in prayer or even by writing to God in a journal if that helps. The key is to learn to process your emotions, thoughts, and pain in Him and allow Him to change you.

CHAPTER 4

Strength for Each Day

"A faithful God does not expect you to do what you cannot; He supplies the needed strength."
~ Erwin W. Lutzer

How do we keep going forward when we have lost everything? Where do we find the strength to wake up and get out of bed, much less carry on with our lives? Each one of us gets tired and worn down. Everyday life has a way of sneaking up on us. Work demands, parenting demands, and just taking care of the day-to-day grind can add up fast. A good nap, trip to the spa, or extra cup of coffee usually will do the trick to get us going. I like to call these switching gears: walking away from the task at hand and taking a break. A stroll around the neighborhood and a quick window-shopping trip are a couple of my favorite ways to take my mind off it all. Hobby Lobby can do wonders! Then I can come back and get things done.

However, there is a different kind of strength we need when tragedy happens. When we get the call we never saw coming. When we get that diagnosis we thought only happens to people in their old age. When we lose all trust in our spouse. When we lose someone very close to us. When all our emotional strength is zapped, and we can't just snap out of it. When the world is falling apart around us and our last thought before we close our eyes and our first thought when we wake up is the unthinkable situation and all we feel is the heavy blanket of grief.

How do we muster up strength in this place? I don't really believe we can on our own. Possibly for a moment, but the reality is this yoke is way too heavy to remove on our own, much less cart around and unpack. This yoke weighs us down and sometimes paralyzes us. It can leave us with no strength to engage in the day to day. Depression looms over us. Panic over leaving the house sets in. Physical symptoms from trauma begin to take root. The reality of not having any control in our lives feels overwhelming. Our will to live is just not there. It takes everything we have to get out of bed and take a shower; past that, forget it. Some of us bear the scars of trauma and tragedy our whole lives, and it turns into debilitating anxiety or anger or bitterness. Sometimes we just don't bounce back.

There is a strength; however, that is supernatural. One that brings true healing and wholeness again. One that breaks us free from the bondage that the enemy wants to trap us in. Let's look at 2 Corinthians 12:9, where the Lord said to Paul, "'My grace is sufficient for you, for my power is made perfect in weakness.' Therefore I will boast all the more gladly about my weaknesses, so that Christ's power may rest on me." God is saying He has everything we need to overcome our circumstances. Jesus is giving us His grace to sustain us. Not only do we receive His grace, but in our weakness His power rests on us! His power is what supernaturally strengthens us to carry on.

This is not some self-help, fake-it-till-you-make-it idea. It's not something we can manifest if we think it enough. This is the actual presence of Jesus Christ resting on us. I call it my daily breath. When I breathe Him in, my focus becomes His peace and my physical and emotional states shift. In times of struggle and pain we must learn to live with Jesus moment by moment. Each breath, each setback, and each day with Jesus. One day at a time, until we are strong enough to step back out there. Jesus sits with us, cries with us, holds us, and walks us through it. Give Jesus the yoke you are carrying that keeps you weighted down in bondage, and He will put His spirit on you and in you to strengthen your steps.

Living with Jesus moment by moment is how we walk through heartache, holding His hand. As we begin conversations with Him throughout the day and process what we are feeling, we begin to surrender our pain in His very capable hands. Reading the Bible daily, wallpapers our mind with His living and active truths. Offering our weaknesses to Him and telling Him how much we need Him, produces humility. Waiting on Him to speak, attunes our ears to hear Him better. Worshipping Him throughout the pain helps us to cry out to God and praise Him instead of focusing solely on the situation.

When we worship and spend time in God's Word, we come to know Him personally and intimately, not just intellectually or based on what others tell us about Him. We get to know Him as our peace, our strength, our grace, our mercy, our hope, our provision, our everything—one moment at a time. Here in this place, we make room for Jesus because without Him we know we don't have enough strength to keep going.

Day by day we learn to surrender, breathe in Jesus's peace, and build our trust in Him. In Matthew 11:28–30, Jesus says, "Come to me, all who weary and burdened, and I will give you rest. Take my yoke upon you and learn from me, for I am gentle and humble in heart, and you will find rest for your souls. For my yoke is easy and my burden is light." Again, Jesus invites us to be with Him. He says, "Come to me." He gives us rest when we come. When we abide in Him, we live life from a place of deep rest.

I had a vision one time where I walked up to a cottage and knocked on the door. Jesus opened the door and took the suitcases I was carrying and set them by the door. He walked me over to a kitchen table that had food laid out and invited me to sit down with Him. As I sat in the chair, He hopped up on the side of the table and began talking to me, just like a friend would. He had a huge smile on His face. I noticed the suitcases by the door, and He saw my concern. He said, "Don't worry about unpacking those now. I will help you unpack each one when it's time." Instead, He invited me to rest and enjoy His presence. Jesus was not in a rush. He wanted us to enjoy our time together so I could rest and build my strength in His presence before we started unpacking. Jesus has a way of helping us "unpack our baggage" when it is time. He knows what we need most.

Philippians 4:19 states, "And my God will meet all your needs according to the riches of his glory in Christ Jesus." I love this scripture so much. God never questions whether His power and presence is enough for us. He knows it is, but we also must trust it to be. Anything we could possibly need in this world we can find in Him alone. Nothing is exempt, including our suffering. Jesus's compassion for us is enough to bring us through completely healed. We need to trust this.

Are you convinced that you don't want to move on or be healed? This might be a weird question for some to admit. I remember feeling this way after Brennen died. I believed if I allowed myself to be happy or move on, then somehow I would forget about him or dishonor what we went through. This feeling brought with it guilt, fear, and anxiety. But these feelings are not from God. These feelings were my own flesh and lack of trust in God as well as the enemy's voice trying to trap me in bondage. The apostle Peter warned us in 1 Peter 5:8 to "Be alert and of sober mind. Your enemy the devil prowls around like a roaring lion looking for someone to devour." Did you know that Satan has a plan for your life? The devil had me slated for destruction, but God had a different plan for me. I had to learn to shut the enemy's mouth and tune in to God's voice speaking over my life. I had to go to the secret place with God.

Psalm 91:1 states "Whoever dwells in the shelter of the Most High will rest in the shadow of the Almighty." Where is this secret place? Jesus is the secret place. He is the shelter that has been prepared for us. Here we are hidden; it's a safe place to come to when we are weak and wounded by our circumstances. Here is where we process our heartaches—through communion and fellowship with Jesus, allowing His supernatural protection to activate—and here is where we will learn to walk again. Here is where freedom and purpose begin to merge from our pain. In the secret place we are always aware of His presence with us.

The night before Jesus went to the cross, what was He doing? How was He processing His grief? He was praying with God, His Father. Matthew 26:36–39 says,

> Then Jesus went with his disciples to a place called Gethsemane, and he said to them, "Sit here while I go over there and pray." He took Peter and the two sons of Zebedee along with him, and he began to be sorrowful and troubled. Then he said to them, "My soul is overwhelmed with sorrow to the point of death. Stay here and keep watch with me." Going a little farther, he fell with his face to the ground and prayed, "My Father, if it is possible, may this cup be taken from me. Yet not as I will, but as you will."

Remember, in Jesus's suffering on the cross, He was accomplishing the will of Father God. When we suffer in Christ and with Him, His will can be worked through us because suffering is the best way to replace our selfish desires with the plans God has for us. Our bags can be unpacked, and in their place, we can be filled with Jesus and all that He has for us. God didn't take away the suffering endured on the cross. Jesus surrendered to it. In His surrender, God gave Jesus the wisdom to see the bigger picture and the strength to endure for a greater purpose. Jesus overcame the grave and was resurrected. We, too, experience a resurrection when we die to ourselves through our suffering. We emerge purified and changed by His strength that now lives in us.

Jesus is our safe place, our resting place, and our hiding place. Jesus enables us to press ahead and overcome things by His strength. Philippians 4:13 states, "I can do all this through him who gives me strength." Exodus 15:2 (NLT) says, "The LORD is my strength and my song; he has given me victory. This is my God, and I will praise him." We find victory through Jesus, and this is something to be joyful about! In the book of Psalms, we read about how King David went through so many trials and sufferings in his life. He was honest about his feelings to God. He had moments of doubt, fear, and frustration, but he worshipped and praised God despite it all.

What did David learn about God through all these trying times? In Psalms 28:7, David declares, "The LORD is my strength and my shield; my heart trusts in him, and he helps me. My heart leaps for joy, and with my song I praise him." He learned that God was his strength! I love that David shared that his heart triumphed! Oh, that our hearts would triumph over every heartache we encounter this side of heaven.

How can we know this strength will hold us up? I know it's our human nature to want a quick fix. We want the shorthand version. Just tell me what to do in three easy steps. Time and relationships don't work like this. God is inviting us into something more than an easy fix. We are being called into communion with the Holy Spirit who lives in us. Jesus sent the Holy Spirit to be our Helper, Comforter, Counselor, Advocate, Intercessor, Reminder and Strengthener. The Holy Spirit in us produces lasting fruit in our lives. When we walk hand in hand with Him and let His wisdom and counsel take root in us, we will see lasting healing. Deep roots take time to grow.

Listen to Paul's perspective when walking through hard times. Paul prayed to take it away, then accepted what was happening, and eventually changed his mind-set on how to handle it. Second Corinthians 12:8–10 says, "Three times I pleaded with the Lord to take it away from me. But he said to me, 'My grace is sufficient for you, for my power is made perfect in weakness.' Therefore I will boast all the more gladly about my weaknesses, so that Christ's power may rest on me. That is why, for Christ's sake, I delight in weaknesses, in insults, in hardships, in persecutions, in difficulties. For when I am weak, then I am strong."

The first part of Paul's prayer may sound familiar: God, please take it away! But then he listened to God's response, not necessarily what he wanted to hear perhaps, but ultimately turned it around to be glad for the suffering because it was here that God made him strong. It's here that God makes us strong too! When we realize the power of God in us and understand that when we are weak, He is strong, then we can rest in this place and know that He will sustain us just like He did Paul.

Let's think about that scripture from this point of view. It says Christ's power rests on us. God taught the Jewish people in the Old Testament about their need for a sabbath rest. This orders our week and allows us to have rest for our bodies but also to spend quality, focused time with God. When Jesus arrived on the scene, He became all believers' ultimate rest. When we become born again and the Holy Spirit lives in us, we have entered His rest. The burden is gone, the striving is gone, the heavy lifting is gone. It's the power of the Holy Spirit in us that allows us to rest in Jesus and obtain His peace. We are quieted from the chaos of the world and our personal problems. Jesus is our constant sabbath.

The strength of Jesus holding us and the power of the Holy Spirit in us is all we need to carry us abundantly through anything we face. As we move into the next chapter, let's discuss faith's role in our journey of trading our pain for a life of freedom and purpose with Jesus. Not only are we grabbing ahold of God's hand and surrendering our hurts, but we are also going to discover faith. God says we cannot please Him without faith in who He is. So, how does faith fit into our pain and suffering? Let's find out. It might just be the key you are missing.

Reflection

Use the scriptures I have shared in this chapter or find others and begin writing them down where you can see them every day. Turn them into prayers and declare them as promises for your life. Watch how Jesus becomes your strength, carries your burdens, renews your mind, and brings triumph to your heart. Watch how He becomes your stronghold and puts the enemy's plans under your feet.

CHAPTER 5

Faith Is Our Key

*"Faith is deliberate confidence in the character of God
whose ways you may not understand at the time."*
~ Oswald Chambers

How can we have faith in God when our world has just been turned upside down? On our journey of processing loss and suffering in the presence of Jesus and having our perspective changed by His Word, we are going to need a key that unlocks the door to our greater purpose and inheritance in Jesus. This key is called faith. The problem is that during pain and heartache any faith we ever had before was crushed; everything we thought we knew and believed was dismantled and left in pieces.

Faith is becoming such a buzzword in our culture. It's been watered down and is often not even worthy of our attention. But I want to pull it front and center for you. You couldn't hop in your car and try to turn it on and drive off without your key, right? Well, God wants us to connect with Him using our faith key to move us in the right direction to our freedom and healing.

If we have not used our key of faith to open the door and peek into the realm of possibility—where Jesus is—we might stay stuck in our heartache and painful experiences. Faith is much more than a cute word written on our sweatshirt. It's a key that unlocks healing and surrendering with Jesus. If we don't understand what faith does, we may stay stuck. Like a car, we must stick the key in the ignition and turn it on!

Jesus handed me and you a key to life in Him with the word *faith* written on it. You might want to pull it out of your pocket right now, because it's a turning point. What is faith anyway? In simple terms, faith is having complete trust or confidence in someone or something. It could also mean loyalty to God. How can we have complete trust and confidence in God? Faith starts by reading the Word of God and surrendering our lives to God and being in prayer. This is where faith is born. Believing what God's word says and trusting in it is faith. Talking to God about what we are going through keeps us close to Him, so we can hear His voice and adhere to His ways. There is so much to learn about faith.

Our faith is supposed to be complete trust in who Jesus is and what He says. The Bible tells us in Hebrews 11:6, "And without faith it is impossible to please God, because anyone who comes to him must believe that he exists and that he rewards those who earnestly seek Him." This truth declares we cannot please God if we do not operate in faith! We must believe in Him to move forward.

Think about a healthy parent-child relationship. A child trusts their parent to take care of everything in their world. They don't typically worry about where their food is coming from or where they are going to get money to buy the latest toy. Every need is supplied by their parents. They have faith that their parent will be there when they get hurt and to watch over them while they sleep. They don't fret over anything. This is childlike faith, and it's how God would love for us to live. Jesus said, "Truly I tell you, unless you change and become like little children, you will never enter the kingdom of heaven. Therefore, whoever takes the lowly position of this child is the greatest in the kingdom of heaven" (Matthew 18:3–4). In other words, faith is the best posture to have, trusting God for everything. This is how we walk in the joy of the Lord.

Let's talk about what faith looks like right now for you, because faith is going to take you far on your journey with Jesus. If we want to catch sight of our circumstance through the lens of Jesus, we will need faith to do so. We need faith to look past how we feel today and into the realm of where Jesus is calling us to. We need faith to grab ahold of Jesus's hand and to trust Him with our hurts, our hearts, and our lives. We need faith to believe God loves us and is for us. Faith infiltrates everything. Our pain and heartache can make our spiritual eyes cloudy—our perception can be hindered. Faith will help our vision of the future to include hope and purpose; our vision will not stay cloudy. Faith is how we are going to discern what to do from here on out. With faith we will begin to comprehend God's promises, His possibilities, and what He can do—not what we can or can't do. How is your faith right now?

Faith has nothing to do with the logical and everything to do with the impossible. Remember, faith is our key to unlock what God wants for us, including but not limited to peace, perspective, healing, freedom, and purpose. There are two types of faith the Bible talks about. Let's explore them.

The first kind of faith is described as the size of a mustard seed. Doesn't seem like much, right? How can a tiny faith produce anything? Our faith journey may start off small but expect great things to grow from it. As Matthew 17:20 says, "Because you have so little faith. Truly I tell you, if you have faith as small as a mustard seed, you can say to this mountain, 'Move from here to there,' and it will move. Nothing will be impossible for you." Jesus said that it doesn't take much faith to move a mountain. But what we put our faith in is the actual key. So, it's not the quantity or strength of our faith; it's the object in which we put our faith. And that object should be Jesus.

We should not despise small beginnings. If you've been a believer for some time, think back to when you first met Jesus. You knew in your heart you were being called into something bigger, but you didn't really know how big; you just decided to step out with your tiny mustard seed of faith and say yes to Jesus. Luke 16:10 teaches us that those who can be trusted with a little can be trusted with much more.

Maybe you're here just looking for anything that can help you not drown in your circumstance; you're not sure about this whole Jesus thing yet. Well, it only takes a small leap of faith for you too. We all start with this small step into trusting Jesus. As intended, this mustard seed of faith in Jesus is planted deep in us and begins to grow over time into a huge, lush mustard tree of faith.

When we plant seeds, they need enough light, water, and fertilizer to grow deep roots into a beautiful plant, vegetable, or flower. This takes time and pruning. Sometimes weeds grow and try to choke out the plant by stealing its nutrients. This is what happens to our faith—something traumatic hits us and tries to choke out our faith, stealing what little we may have had. When we allow the worries and events in our lives to steal our faith in God, we become hopeless and stuck. In our weakness, when our faith is gone, the enemy comes and steals from us too. The enemy destroys our belief in God and tries to steal our salvation. Let's read Luke 8:4–15 to grasp what Jesus says about this circumstance:

> While a large crowd was gathering and people were coming to Jesus from town after town, he told this parable: "A farmer went out to sow his seed. As he was scattering the seed, some fell along the path; it was trampled on, and the birds ate it up. Some fell on rocky ground, and when it came up, the plants withered because

they had no moisture. Other seed fell among thorns, which grew up with it and choked the plants. Still other seed fell on good soil. It came up and yielded a crop, a hundred times more than was sown." When he said this, he called out, "Whoever has ears to hear, let them hear." His disciples asked him what this parable meant. He said, "The knowledge of the secrets of the kingdom of God has been given to you, but to others I speak in parables, so that, 'though seeing, they may not see; though hearing, they may not understand.' This is the meaning of the parable: The seed is the word of God. Those along the path are the ones who hear, and then the devil comes and takes away the word from their hearts, so that they may not believe and be saved. Those on the rocky ground are the ones who receive the word with joy when they hear it, but they have no root. They believe for a while, but in the time of testing they fall away. The seed that fell among thorns stands for those who hear, but as they go on their way they are choked by life's worries, riches and pleasures, and they do not mature. But the seed on good soil stands for those with a noble and good heart, who hear the word, retain it, and by persevering produce a crop."

Where we plant our seed of faith matters. We must plant it in Jesus, who is the Word of God. In Him, we plant it in good soil where the devil can't steal it, where it can grow deep and withstand the storms of life.

In 2020, when we were stuck at home, I finally found the time to plant a garden, something I've always wanted to do. Some of my family planted huge gardens when I was growing up, but I didn't know much about the process because I had never planted a garden on my own. So, my husband built me raised garden beds in the backyard and put in the "right soil," as he said after doing some research. Then I planted some seeds and some plants. I casually stepped out in faith to see what would happen. After watering it and pulling some weeds, I surprisingly grew a very abundant garden that year. In fact, people started asking me to show them how to plant a garden because mine looked so vibrant and fruitful. Honestly, I did the basics of gardening and just trusted that the seed I could no longer see would bloom. Think about it: we plant a tiny seed in the ground, in dark soil, and we add some water and sunlight, and it miraculously grows into food to eat. That little seed appears nothing like the fruit it grows into!

Faith is a lot like growing a garden. We can't perceive at first what will bloom from a tiny seed of faith planted by trust in Jesus. However, the seed we plant must be taken care of. This is how our faith will grow over time with Jesus. As we read His Word, pray, live in community, and trust Him through it all, our faith grows deep roots and becomes lush and beautiful and fruitful.

The following year I planted the garden again, but that year we experienced a drought in our area, and I got too busy and distracted to care for it, and well, you know, the seeds I planted died, and my garden beds became overgrown with weeds. This is what happens to us when the weeds of life start to appear and grow—they steal the harvest and we become discouraged and give up the hard work. We begin to die from the harsh conditions. Herein comes the enemy hoping to use these difficult situations to choke the life out of us. If we are not careful, we will wither up like my garden did. We need to see that faith is the key that unlocks our ability to stay close to Jesus and walk out the other side. But we must keep our faith alive and safe just like the garden. Faith that He will heal us. Faith that He will bring purpose from the pain. Faith that He will bring peace. Faith that He will bring life back. Faith that Jesus will do the impossible.

Each of us needs to plant a mustard seed of faith into our hard stories. We must bring our seemingly impossible pain into the realm of what Jesus can do. Faith will bloom into trust that He will bring us through to the other side. Faith will keep us close to His presence. Faith with bring alive the promises in the Bible. We might not know exactly how our faith will grow through this process—just like that seed I planted in my garden—but it will produce some kind of harvest as we bury it deep in God's Word, water it with prayer, and wait with expectation as it grows stronger and bigger in the hand of Jesus. Our faith may start out the size of a mustard seed, but it will grow into a huge mustard tree that can provide shade for others on their long, hot journey through pain. The seed of faith planted in our pain can lead us into the freedom that another person caught in a nightmare needs. We can tell them and show them how Jesus can help them also. We can invite them to grab ahold of Jesus's hand too.

The second kind of faith I want to share about is a gift of the Holy Spirit. There are multiple gifts of the Spirit. These gifts are how the Holy Spirit works through us to edify and strengthen others. They are supernatural giftings that Jesus baptizes us in so that the Holy Spirit's power can work through us. There are nine gifts according to 1 Corinthians 12. These include the word of knowledge, faith, healing, miracles, prophecy, discerning of spirits, speaking in tongues, and interpretation of tongues. The Holy Spirit can and will use these gifts as needed to help and encourage others. I want to focus on the gift of faith. As such, we can receive the "gift of faith."

How are faith the size of a mustard seed and the gift of faith different? We need the "mustard seed" to take the step to meet Jesus in our pain, and it's also what we need to step out and meet Him for the first time—called saving faith. The gift of faith, however, is having a supernatural ability to discern in the spirit the plans and purposes of God. To believe in what He can do despite what we see. This kind of faith is a supernatural manifestation of the Spirit of God. This gift of faith enables us to have complete assurance in who Jesus is. We can see in the realm of possibility. There are many examples of this in the Bible. Let's explore a few.

In 1 Kings 17:1, the prophet Elijah had prayed for rain to stop, to cause a drought: "As the LORD, the God of Israel, lives, whom I serve, there will be neither dew nor rain in the next few years except at my word." Then He began to pray for it to rain again at the right time. First Kings 18:44 states, "The seventh time the servant reported, 'A cloud as small as a man's hand is rising from the sea.' So Elijah said, 'Go and tell Ahab, "Hitch up your chariot and go down before the rain stops you."'" Elijah had the assurance of rain before it even rained. Elijah had the gift of faith.

God specializes in the impossible. This kind of faith displays an unshakable trust that no matter what something seems like (drought), God is going to come through somehow (send rain). This kind of faith doesn't grasp life from the stance of failure but from a place of victory, where God wants us to be. The gift of faith often occurs as a deep knowing. From this deep knowing comes extraordinary trust, faith, and confidence in God. Ask the Holy Spirit for the gift of faith so that you can believe for a future filled with healing and freedom from pain. Set your eyes and faith beyond what it feels like in the moment. The Holy Spirit will work through you to demonstrate God's power to encourage, strengthen, and empower others to move forward in God.

And then there was Noah! Can you imagine the kind of faith Noah needed to build the ark? No one had ever even seen rain. Plus, it took him 120 years of building and waiting for this flood to come. We know waiting can be hard! To top it off, every step of Noah's journey came with ridicule and judgment from others. How did he persevere? Noah walked in the supernatural gift of faith. This enabled him to do the impossible.

I'm sure Noah got tired and experienced days when he questioned it all, but he did not give up. Hebrews 11:7 says, "By faith Noah, when warned about things not yet seen, in holy fear built an ark to save his family. By his faith he condemned the world and became heir of the righteousness that is in keeping with faith." Did you see it? It was by faith and reverence that Noah did what he did. He trusted God and feared Him—and mankind was spared.

We can't forget Abraham who was told he would be the father of many nations. He was old, and he and his wife didn't even have a child. But he trusted that God calls those things which are not as though they were. Romans 4:17–18 starts in the middle of a thought and states, "(as it is written: 'I have made you a father of many nations') He is our father in the sight of God, in whom he believed-the God who gives life to the dead and calls into being things that were not. Against all hope, Abraham in hope believed and so became the father of many nations, just as it had been said to him, 'So shall your offspring be.'" Although Abraham didn't get to see "many nations" born to him, he received the promise through the seemingly impossible birth of his son, Isaac, that indeed it would happen someday.

Jesus is inviting us into a life of supernatural faith—where we are not defined by our circumstances. The enemy wants to steal our purpose and make as a victim for the rest of our lives. But just like the examples in the Bible above, are we not called to so much more? We do not need to suffer as those without hope. By faith, as followers of Christ, we will take up our cross and our suffering and lay them at the feet of Jesus and walk away with purpose and a greater faith that will move mountains and be a testimony to later share with others.

How do we begin to step out in faith, much less ask for the gift of faith? It all begins with—you guessed it—prayer! These are our conversations with Jesus. This is where we work it out and get the new blueprints for our lives. Ask Jesus for this gift for your impossible situation. James 4:2 tells us, "Yet you don't have what you want because you don't ask God for it." Prayer is always the foundation where faith is planted. Take a journal, go inside your closet, put on worship music, and begin to talk to God. This is the place where our messy becomes God's beautiful. It helps to have the right motive in our prayers as well. If we align our hearts with God's heart, this allows our motives to be His will. The best way to know if you are in God's will is to pray for God's will to happen in your situation, not your own will. God often wants something else for us than we want for ourselves.

You may not see it yet, but your story has a greater purpose. When we pray for God's will and not our own, it gives God the glory, and it will point others to Jesus so they may experience His love and salvation and they, too, can walk out of their pain and into freedom. When others hear your healing story, it gives them hope and courage to step out in faith, with the thought that if Jesus can do that for you, then just maybe Jesus can do that for them. The Bible says we overcome "by the blood of the Lamb and by the word of their testimony" (Revelation 12:11). Our story has power. And guess what? Here is where our purpose from the pain begins: it's in this moment of realization that we begin to experience new life, new beginnings, and a greater faith ready to be shared with others.

I was given the opportunity to go on a mission trip a while back. I never dreamed that I would go to another country and share my story of Jesus's healing after I lost my son. Each time I got to share my story; it spoke to hurting people. It became a sacred moment. The looks on their faces, tears in their eyes, and the hugs that came afterward were priceless. My story gave them hope in Jesus. My story helped them understand that they are not alone. They felt seen by God in that moment knowing that someone would come all the way from America to their remote dirt-floor home and as I shared my story of pain and suffering, they became encouraged in their painful stories too. It didn't matter that we spoke different languages or that I came from the city and they, indigenous Indians, lived in the mountains and jungles of Mexico. Pain and suffering are part of a universal language.

These people, who are also loved by God, got to see His power in my pain. They got to experience the Father's heart, and in return their faith grew! This is my hope for each of you too. That you feel seen by God, who created you, loves you, and wants more for you than you can imagine!

Hold close to this scripture in Hebrews 11:1–3: "Now faith is confidence in what we hope for and assurance about what we do not see. This is what the ancients were commended for. By faith we understand that the universe was formed at God's command, so that what is seen was not made out of what was visible." Faith is our key! We cannot please God without faith. We will move our mountains of pain into the purposes of the kingdom of God when we choose faith. Faith leads us to redemption, restoration, healing, and freedom. When our faith is tested, let's remember James 1:2–4, "Consider it pure joy, my brothers and sisters, whenever you face trials of many kinds, because you know that the testing of your faith produces perseverance. Let perseverance finish its work so that you may be mature and complete, not lacking anything."

So far on our journey we have seen our need to invite Jesus into our pain and suffering and to live intentionally in His presence, understanding what the Father's heart is for us, relying on Jesus's supernatural strength and picking up our key of faith. We are on our way to having our pain exchanged for purpose in the kingdom of God! Let's continue the journey and see what happens when we trade our shaky confidence for an unshakable God-confidence.

Reflection

Now, let's get real with ourselves for a moment. Are we finding other ways to deal with the pain life throws at us? Any habits or patterns we've picked up along the way to numb our feelings instead of allowing Jesus to heal them? If you're not sure, no biggie; just ask the Holy Spirit to shine a light into your heart to reveal it. Remember, prayer is the foundation for faith to move mountains. It's like having a heart-to-heart with God, letting Him in on your struggles and asking for a little guidance. You can pour out your heart to Him and get it off your chest. Trust me, it makes a world of difference.

Let's pick up a tiny seed of faith that you'll sow in the rich soil of your connection with Jesus today, aiming for your healing and freedom. Take a moment to reflect and bring it to Him in prayer.

CHAPTER 6

God-Confidence

"Self-confidence has limited potential. God-confidence has unlimited possibility."
~ Renee Swope

D o you struggle with self-doubt or feelings of inadequacy, or are you one of those people who are crazy confident in their abilities? No matter how we feel about ourselves, we all have one thing in common: each of us needs to learn how to surrender our lack of confidence or our overconfidence in ourselves for the confidence we can only find in Jesus Christ.

I admit I've always been one to struggle with confidence. I have always felt inadequate or like I am missing something everyone else knows. I tend to hold back and play it safe, second-guessing whether I have what it takes. I also tend to hide behind others, where it's comfortable. The problem with this is I'm focusing on myself and not what God can do through me. Over the years, the Holy Spirit has taught me that I need to "do it afraid." I can trust the Holy Spirit to show up for me when I step out into the fear of the unknown. But this requires action from me. A faith-based confidence that has nothing to do with my feelings and everything to do with what I know to be true of God: He shows up!

I've met others over the years who seem to have the opposite problem. They are overly confident in their own abilities and don't allow or trust God or anyone else to help. This breeds pride and often an identity crisis when they crash and burn. Neither extreme is healthy nor honoring to Jesus. The solution for both is building our confidence in who Jesus is and who we are in Him.

This chapter is about trading our self-reliance or lack thereof for a confidence that goes beyond ourselves. When we walk through times of sorrow and heartache, our confidence can become devastated. Our identity may even begin to take on the form of what we went through. When we find ourselves in this vulnerable place, we feel exposed and stripped of all we know. Are you an open wound walking around in need of healing?

If you said yes to that question, picture this: a path where the spotlight shifts from the shaky ground beneath your feet to the unshakable foundation of God's truths. Let's unpack the narrative of confidence—not in our own might but in the unwavering strength that comes when we lean on someone far greater—a confidence in God that eclipses any doubt we might have about ourselves. As we struggle with trials and suffering in this lifetime, we find that when the rug is pulled out from underneath our feet, we are faced with one reality: we are not in control.

This reality leaves us questioning who we are and everything we thought we understood about life. It's the beginning of a paradigm shift. Our previous reality is no longer valid. The question of whether we were confident in ourselves before fades away. As we are slipping, we can continue to fall or steady ourselves on a firm foundation.

Let's explore the kind of confidence that's rooted in the divine nature of Jesus, the one who is asking you to take His hand to steady you. This confidence is tailor-made for each of us—it's a journey into the heart of confidence, but with a twist. We learn to step out from the shadows of self-doubt or self-reliance into the radiant light fueled by an unshakable belief in God. This is not a confidence in our own abilities but stems from the grace of God. To do this we must be honest with ourselves. Where do you fall on the spectrum of God-confidence?

What do the Scriptures say about being confident in Jesus? Jeremiah 17:7 (NLT) says, "But blessed are those who trust in the LORD and have made the LORD their hope and confidence." Psalm 27:3 says, "Though an army besiege me, my heart will not fear; though war break out against me, even then I will be confident." Psalm 118:6 says, "The Lord is with me; I will not be afraid. What can mere mortals do to me?"

There are so many scriptures in the Bible that speak about putting our full confidence in Jesus. These are only a few. It's one thing to read these scriptures, but it's another thing for them to become a part of how we think and approach life as well. The confidence we can experience in God can become our identity and a part of who we are. Let's look at the God-confidence Jesus carried during His earthly ministry.

Jesus held an unwavering confidence in the purpose of the gospel message. He believed that the gospel redeemed God's people and had the power to save all who believed. Jesus is the gospel message. Jesus wasn't and isn't blind to suffering. He possesses compassion for us. He stood on God's truths and His purposes and plans for mankind. He did not waver in this mission, and despite all He went through, His confidence remained. Jesus was sent out like a perfectly released arrow with the purposes of God for all mankind. Jesus walked humbly, not arrogantly. He realized the plans of the Father were not based on human ability but on the power of our Father's love for us.

Jesus saw the beginning, the middle, and the end of humanity's story. Jesus understood the bigger picture. He didn't base His feelings or actions on the condition of the world; he wasn't consumed with our failures or the schemes of the enemy. He didn't let the suffering

He endured detour His confidence in who God is. He grasped that He, in fact, came for our redemption and restoration, which was extended by God. His mission was to restore and take back the territory that the kingdom of darkness had infiltrated. Jesus trusted God's plan and was confident that nothing would change it or stop it.

Jesus is still very aware of the condition of mankind. He never once suggested that any of us were too far gone in our sin and flesh or hurt and pain for His sacrifice to heal and change us. Jesus rightfully claimed healing and salvation for us, no matter how far we might go astray. His confidence is in the work of the cross, which was God's plan all along.

Our confidence is shaken when we take our eyes off Jesus and allow them to become fixated on our problems. Jesus's confidence flowed from Himself by first loving God and following His commands and obeying His will, and then in turn His love flowed to others, which is God's motivation for it all—His love for us. We, too, can live entirely confident when we choose to love, live, and trust God's plan as Jesus did. Jesus sustained confidence in the plan even though it required Him to suffer. Jesus did not get off the cross, but God saw His plan through as He had promised. We can rest in knowing that God will be with us in our sufferings and will bring us through as well.

All right, that's great that Jesus had confidence in God—after all, He is fully God and fully man! But how do we stand on that same confidence that Jesus did, especially when life throws us curveballs? We can start by ditching the solo act and leaning hard into relying on Him, not our own shaky foundation. Let's swap out those feelings of inadequacy, insecurity, and self-doubt that trials, hurts, and disappointments bring up in us, for a bold confidence in Jesus Christ. When we trade our hurts for who Jesus says we are, we can rest in the confidence that God is on our side and working through our pain.

Here's the deal: we're not showing up with confidence in our own abilities (or lack thereof). No, we're standing strong, wholly submitted to God's will, understanding that our strength is like a toddler trying to lift a truck. And we all know how toddlers throw fits when things are hard. We don't have to be the superheroes in our stories or others; it's about being confident that God is the ultimate orchestrator, working through us to unveil His plans.

The secret to our confidence in Jesus is found in two scriptures. John 15:5 tells us, "I am the vine; you are the branches. If you remain in me and I in you, you will bear much fruit; apart from me you can do nothing." And Philippians 4:13 says, "I can do all this through him who gives me strength." What are these verses showing us? For one, we cannot do anything of eternal value without Jesus, but with Him we can do all things. Not some things, *all* things! Whatever we do in our own capacity carries the potential to fall apart or, worse, not have any significance in eternity.

What's the point of being rich and famous in this world in our own strength and desires just to have it all burned up in the fire at the end of time? What's the point of living on the sidelines, too scared to step out because of our own lack of confidence, and then one day have a heart full of what-ifs and regrets? God balances out our lack of confidence with His strength and our overconfidence with our need for Him. In both situations, when we let God in, we are humbled yet also made bold in Christ. The hard things that we walk through, the assignments we are entrusted with, can only be accomplished in Jesus. It's never about us and our abilities. It's about obeying the will of God for our lives—the good, the bad, and the ugly.

When we say, "I can't do this, God," but trust that God will help see it through, we can rest in the confidence of Jesus. If we stay stuck in our lack of abilities or allow suffering to keep us from moving forward, we waste opportunities to help others and lose out on what

God has for our lives, *even though* we suffered. It's just suffering to suffer. Isn't confidence in God starting to sound good?

Have you ever heard of Daniel in the Bible? In Daniel 6 we learn that a trap was set for him. He was favored by the king, and others didn't like it. They wanted to get rid of him. During Daniel's time, the king of Babylon, Darius, to whom Daniel was of service, was tricked into signing a law that would put to death anyone who worshipped any god other than the king himself. Daniel was firm on praying and worshipping the one true God, no matter what the law said. When Daniel was caught praying and the others brought the news to the king, he realized what had happened. Daniel would have to be thrown into the lions' den as his punishment.

What can we learn from Daniel? First, he had God's confidence to stand on. He was so confident in God no matter the outcome. Do you trust in God no matter the outcome? Let's find out what happened to Daniel.

Daniel 6:16–17 says, "So the king gave the order, and they brought Daniel and threw him into the lions' den. The king said to Daniel, 'May your God, whom you serve continually, rescue you!' A stone was brought and placed over the mouth of the den, and the king sealed it with his own signet ring and with the rings of his nobles, so that Daniel's situation might not be changed." Then the king left and went home but couldn't eat or sleep with worry over Daniel. In the morning the king ran to the den and called out in anguish, "Daniel, servant of the living God, has your God, whom you serve continually, been able to rescue you from the lions?" (Daniel 6:20). Daniel answered, "May the king live forever! My God sent his angel, and he shut the mouths of the lions. They have not hurt me" (Daniel 6:21–22). Verse 23 continues, "The king was overjoyed and gave orders to lift Daniel out of the den. And when Daniel was lifted from the den, no wound was found on him, because he had trusted in his God." Then King Darius wrote to all the nations and peoples of every language in all the earth saying, "May you prosper greatly! I issue a decree that in every part of my kingdom people must fear and reverence the God of Daniel. For he is the living God and he endures forever; his kingdom will not be destroyed, his dominion will never end. He rescues and he saves; he performs signs and wonders in the heavens and on the earth. He has rescued Daniel from the power of the lions" (Daniel 6).

Daniel's confidence in God not only carried him through this ordeal but caused the king of Babylon to take notice of God and issue a decree that everyone had to fear and revere God. Wow! Our confidence in God causes others to take notice. The king was in awe of God, and Daniel prospered because of his obedience and confidence in God.

George Mueller lived in the 1800s and was born in Germany. He spent most of his life in England pastoring a church, but he is mostly known for his orphan ministry. He cared for over ten thousand orphans in his lifetime. He also became a missionary in his seventies. The thing that made George so famous is the confidence he carried in God. He was said to have prayed in millions of dollars in today's currency for the orphans he oversaw, and at the same time, he was known for never asking for any money from anyone. He didn't even take a salary from his church. He prayed, trusted God, and waited on Him to show up, and God did! God would put George's needs on the hearts of individuals, and they would take care of it. He never had to take out a loan or go in debt either! He and the orphans never went hungry; in fact, he built five houses for them! This is amazing God-confidence.

If God can show up for Daniel in the lions' den and for George and the orphans, time and time again supplying their every need, then can't God do the same for us in our heartaches? Nothing is too hard for God. As we build our confidence in God, we make room for the true source of confidence in our lives: Jesus working through us.

We'll have the confidence that He will deliver us from our pain and bring purpose from it, the confidence that He will make all things right at some point, the confidence to trust Him on our healing journey, the confidence to move forward with what He is calling us to, and most importantly the deep confidence and assurance that God is our firm foundation and we will not be shaken to the point of no return when we stand in Him.

Here is some of the fruit we will experience when we build our confidence on the foundation of Jesus:

- We will stand on a firm foundation. Our confidence is built when we know the Word of God and it becomes our measuring stick for how we view the world and our experiences. It never changes or sways with the seasons. Jesus is the same yesterday, today, and tomorrow. We can trust His steadiness. When we do, we will become like "a man building a house, who dug down deep and laid the foundation on the rock. When a flood came, the torrent struck that house but could not shake it, because it was well built" (Luke 6:48).
- We will know that Jesus will never leave us or forsake us. The Holy Spirit lives inside us as our comforter and helper and will remind us of truth. Psalm 139:7–8 says, "Where can I go from your Spirit? Where can I flee from your presence? If I go up to the heavens, you are there; if I make my bed in the depths, you are there."
- We will trust that Jesus will bring beauty from our ashes. Isaiah 66:9 says, "'Do I bring to the moment of birth and not give delivery?' says the Lord. 'Do I close up the womb when I bring to delivery?' says your God." If we wait on Him and give Him time to weave the story and bring forth the fruit, the beauty will shine through.

- <u>We will overcome by the blood of the lamb and the word of our testimony</u>. We need to love others and give them the hope we found in Jesus in our hard places. Let our pain be used to help others, to be the lifeline they need to keep going. Galatians 6:2 says, "Carry each other's burdens, and in this way you will fulfill the law of Christ."
- <u>We will humble ourselves and pray and seek God</u>. Tell Him your feelings and where you have been putting your confidence instead of in Him. We must spend time with Him. Psalm 62:8 says, "Trust in him at all times, you people; pour out your hearts to him, for God is our refuge."
- <u>We will know that God works out things for our good</u>. When we take what we have to offer, however little that is, and give it to Him in faith, He can do the impossible. Luke 18:27 says, "What is impossible with man is possible with God."
- <u>We will find peace</u>. Isaiah 26:3 states, "You will keep in perfect peace those whose minds are steadfast, because they trust in you."
- <u>We will have victory</u>. First Corinthians 15:57 says, "But thanks be to God! He gives us victory through our Lord Jesus Christ."
- <u>We will be certain that God will never let us down</u>. Man will, but God cannot. Be confident that God has your back and will always provide an alternative. First Corinthians 10:13 states, "No temptation has overtaken you except what is common to mankind. And God is faithful; he will not let you be tempted beyond what you can bear. But when you are tempted, he will also provide a way out so that you can endure it."
- <u>We will approach His throne with boldness</u>. Hebrews 4:16 states, "Let us then approach God's throne of grace with confidence, so that we may receive mercy and find grace to

help us in our time of need." We can be confident that God's grace will help us no matter what we face.

- <u>We will learn to wait on God.</u> Don't jump ahead of Him or leave Him out of your life. Give Him time to do what He needs to do. Psalm 27:14 says, "Wait for the LORD; be strong and take heart and wait for the Lord."
- <u>We will live with a heart of gratitude.</u> When we know Jesus, we always have something to be thankful for. First Chronicles 16:34 states, "Give thanks to the Lord, for he is good; his love endures forever."

If you are struggling with doubt that you, too, can walk in this kind of confidence, I want to encourage you. It's not a confidence you have on your own, but it has everything to do with the power of the Holy Spirit in you. We have a constant communion with Jesus because the Holy Spirit lives in us! This is where our power to choose to stand on the confidence of Jesus comes from.

So, let's walk in our God-confidence and shout from the rooftops about who He is and what He is doing in us. Jesus is not just a part of our story—He *is* our story. He's our peace, our freedom, our healer, and the secret to our confidence, even if we have been thrown into what feels like a lions' den! Remember, God's been in the lion's den before! Nothing is too big for Him.

Let's live out this truth. Let's inspire others to trade their shaky confidence for God- confidence. Together, as children of the King, we're standing tall with confidence, shouting, "It's all because of Jesus, and that's where we find our true selves!" Let this new confidence propel us onward to something so much better than this world could ever throw at us. I want to end this chapter with Psalm 16:5–9 and I want you to let it sink deep into your soul:

> Lord, you alone are my portion and my cup;
> you make my lot secure. The boundary lines
> have fallen for me in pleasant places; surely I
> have a delightful inheritance. I will praise the
> Lord, who counsels me; even at night my heart
> instructs me. I keep my eyes always on the Lord.
> With him at my right hand, I will not be shaken.
> Therefore my heart is glad and my tongue
> rejoices; my body also will rest secure.

As we learn to trust God and that His strength is in us, covering our weaknesses, we will not be pummeled by life's storms. We will be deeply rooted to the vine. We will remember who we are in Christ and who He is to us. As we grow in our God-confidence, we will see that it gives us the firm foundation to face anything that comes our way. As we encounter fiery trials in our life, this fire can either burn us down or light us up. In the next chapter, we'll see what I'm talking about.

Reflection

Take a moment to ponder how your life would transform if you swapped out your shaky confidence for the unwavering assurance that only Jesus can provide. Imagine the impact on your daily existence, relationships, and pursuits. Jot down this vivid picture of what life would be like with a rock-solid confidence rooted in Jesus and make a commitment to bring it to God in prayer.

As you embark on this journey, find a scripture that resonates with you, something that becomes more than just words on a page—a belief profoundly rooted in your confidence in Jesus. Commit to memorizing Psalm 16:6–9, letting it be the anchor for your newfound assurance. It's not just about a change in perspective; it's about embracing a confidence that transcends the uncertainties of life, anchored in the unchanging character of Jesus.

CHAPTER 7

Fire Either Burns Us Down or Lights Us Up!

> *"Fiery trials make golden Christians; sanctified*
> *afflictions are spiritual promotions."*
> ~ D.L. Moody

F ire is useful for survival, but at the same time, it can be a force of destruction. Fire keeps us warm, cooks our food, gives us light, and removes trash when controlled. To me, there is nothing better than sitting around a fireplace keeping warm on a cold day and watching the beautiful light the fire gives off. In a fireplace, the fire is controlled and holds a purpose. This brings us beauty and warmth. Fire can also cause a lot of damage. Fire burns down houses and forests and can even take our life. I remember one time lighting a candle that rested in a stand; it fell over before I could catch it. Within seconds it burned up half a picture frame and the picture inside it. Fire is fast! It can instantly spin out of control if we don't have a handle on it.

Not sure if you have ever thought about what fire is but according to *How Stuff Works* the online definition states, "fire comes from a chemical reaction between oxygen in the atmosphere and some sort of fuel. Of course, wood and gasoline don't spontaneously catch on fire just because they're surrounded by oxygen. For the combustion reaction to happen, you have to heat the fuel to its ignition temperature.[3] This is similar to how we can react in a "fiery ordeal," as the Bible describes. The hard things we go through can heat us up and ignite a spark in us that either burns us down or creates a light glowing in the darkness that surrounds us.

Fire contains pressure and transforming power! If you read the Bible enough, you'll begin to see a pattern that God likes to speak to us in nature and common daily life. First Peter 4:12–13 states, "Dear friends, do not be surprised at the fiery ordeal that has come on you to test you, as though something strange were happening to you. But rejoice inasmuch as you participate in the sufferings of Christ, so that you may be overjoyed when his glory is revealed." This verse tells us not to be surprised at the fiery ordeal that has come to test us. This is the pressure we experience in difficult circumstances that burns off what is not Christlike in us.

When Brennen died, it seemed like I was being consumed by a fire. Honestly, it felt like everything inside me was being burned. Thanks to Jesus, He didn't allow me to burn up. Instead, He stayed with me in the fire and allowed it to burn off the things that could no longer be a part of me as a new creation in Christ. Doubt, fear, feeling like a failure, loss of control, and feelings of hopelessness were burned off. His fire could now burn bright within me.

Did you notice that fire does not just *spontaneously* occur? Fire needs the right heat to shine its light. Guess what? So do we! When the fiery trials come upon us, the heat can make us either conform to the pressure that burns off the junk in us, allowing Christ to

---

3   Tom Harris, "How Fire Works," HowStuffWorks.com, accessed March 20, 2024, https://science.howstuffworks.com/environmental/earth/geophysics/fire1.htm.

transform us, or succumb to the burn and get hurt or snuffed out in the process.

How we handle these fiery trials makes all the difference as to where we end up—either burned and bitter or shining bright and transformed, just the light someone else needs in their darkness.

Too many Christians become snuffed out when the heat gets turned up. All that is left is smoldering smoke billowing from them. I've lived my fair share of trials. Satan wants nothing more than to take us down. He wants these trials to make us so weary that we give up. He wants us exhausted from the cares of this life, the fears that surround us, the doubts that plague us, and the heartache that overwhelms us. He wants us to give up on believing we can be healed, free, and delivered. The Bible says, "Let us not become weary in doing good, for at the proper time we will reap a harvest if we do not give up" (Galatians 6:9). Why does the enemy care anyway? Because Scripture says we will reap a harvest in proper time! The enemy doesn't want us to prosper.

Let's face it, people don't want to change for the fun of it. Change is hard. Walking through the fire hurts. We prefer to stay in our safe spaces and comfort zones. I know I do. As we go through life, the enemy of our soul is looking for anything to trip us up and make us fall, never to walk again. He wants to steal, kill, and destroy all that is important to us. God wants the exact opposite.

Genesis 50:20 says, "You intended to harm me, but God intended it for good to accomplish what is now being done, the saving of many lives." God can use these trials for our good, and Satan wants to use them for our demise. But we also must choose. We can choose to become a lifelong victim or seek Jesus to help us work it out. When we choose Jesus, the enemy is defeated. All of us have a decision to make as we navigate the different trials we find ourselves in.

What splendored thing can come out of these trials that God told us about? Let's review Galatians again. God says that we will reap a harvest at the proper time. Does He say instantly? No! The "proper time," or due season, is the key word here. What is happening amid these trials as we are waiting for the proper time? This leads us to the concept of seasons in our life. Seasons come and go. These times carry fiery trials, pain, suffering, heartache, and adversity. They also carry purpose, healing, peace, joy, and character growth. All of us can agree that we can tell a lot about a person when they are under pressure; what's inside eventually springs forth. We will see as our life unfolds, walking gracefully, and taking a hold of the hand of Jesus through every season makes a difference.

Just like the different physical seasons in nature, we also encounter different spiritual seasons in our lives. These periods produce different fruit and help shape our spiritual growth. Surprisingly, the harsh seasons are a part of this process. The harder seasons can be dry and cold with no evidence of fruit or growth in sight, while some bring huge storms where everything is torn upside down. Some bring a time of pruning and replanting seeds. Then there are seasons of abundance and harvest that bring life-giving rain.

All these seasons lead us to the "due season," which is the fulfillment of what God is working out in us. He determines when it is the right moment. Rushing through a difficult season or trying to help it along doesn't usually work out in our favor. We must wait out the storm and see it through to get to the reward. When we try to "help" God along, we tend to take things into our own hands.

A perfect example is when Abraham and Sarah tried to come up with their own plan to have a child instead of waiting on God's promise. Remember God promised Abraham a child and many descendants—as many as the stars in heaven! Sarah was old and just couldn't believe it could happen. So, she devised a plan that ended with her maidservant giving Abraham a son named Ishmael. This turned into a disaster as you can imagine. Eventually God did bring her the rightful, promised son—Isaac—but not without consequences for Ishmael. Her plan didn't turn out well because she took matters into her own hands and didn't wait on the Lord. Luckily nothing can thwart God's plans. Isaac was born, but not without the consequences for her decision.

Therefore, we need to seek God and wait on Him in each season we are facing. This discipline allows our roots to grow deep in the soil of Jesus, so the storms don't blow us over. Here we gain wisdom and revelation, which then propels us into the next season He wants for us.

Some seasons never seem to end, but we must keep trusting and clinging to God despite the circumstances. Everything we go through is preparing us for God's due season! Habakkuk 2:3 says, "For the revelation awaits an appointed time." We will reap only at the proper time!

In these long, difficult seasons, our adversary wants to wear us down. Do you feel worn down? Is the enemy prowling around waiting to devour you? Stay close to God and learn to trust the journey. The fiery ordeals, wilderness times, and storms are temporary. Allow this time to produce the fruit God has for you—good fruit like James 1 describes, such as joy, perseverance, maturity, and wisdom. Have faith that He always shows up! Our due seasons are what we have sown in our prayers, obedience, sacrifices, and staying the course God laid out for us. We experience the reaping and harvest as He works out miracles in our lives that we never saw coming. We begin to sense the shift taking place because after we are filled with what God gave us, it will be poured out to help others in need.

One hard season I vividly remember that made no sense at the time turned out to be one of my fondest memories!

For five years we lived in the beautiful state of Colorado; we loved it there. In fact, we loved it so much we never wanted to leave. It was definitely a joyful, life-giving season of our lives. But then, the still small voice of the Holy Spirit started leading us into another season.

Transitioning from season to season can be hard because it requires obedience and sacrifice. What was God doing?

God was leading us back to Texas and away from Colorado. My family not only loved the state, but we loved our church, the scenery, and our house. Even though it made no sense to us, my husband and I chose to obey, and we moved back to Texas, our home state.

Shortly after returning to Texas, my husband's job did not work out, and we moved again to a different city. Within one and a half years we moved from Colorado Springs to Dallas to San Antonio and finally landed in Austin. None of us were clicking with any of the churches we visited. There was nothing wrong with these churches; they just didn't feel like home to us. Nothing made sense! It felt like we were wandering through the desert with no end in sight.

One night I cried out to the Lord and asked, "Father, did we make a mistake?" I opened my Bible and my eyes "randomly" went to these words in Deuteronomy 1:6–7: "The LORD our God said to us at Horeb, 'You have stayed long enough at this mountain. Break camp and advance into the hill country.'" God was about to send us to Austin, Texas. It's called the Hill Country, for those of you not from Texas! The Holy Spirit made it clear that it wasn't a mistake; we were trading the mountains for the hills. God is always speaking to us if we are listening.

After we decided to move, about a week later a friend of mine in Colorado sent me an email and said, "Hey, in church today, they announced sending a team down to Austin to plant a new church." Did I read that right? My most beloved church was coming to *Austin, Texas*—to where God just happened to be sending us!

I sat down and realized at that moment: we were being sent to help plant that church! I cried my eyes out because I knew if we hadn't been obedient back in Colorado, we would have missed this amazing season we were about to walk into! This season became one of the most treasured memories in my life. The key is, it came out of a difficult season. We were in the middle of a fiery ordeal so that God could prepare us for the next season.

As I mentioned earlier, I love analogies. I love how God speaks to us in common everyday life. All of creation points to Him, even the fire and the seasons. In Ecclesiastes 3:1–8, God lays it all out:

> There is a time for everything, and a season for every activity under the heavens: a time to be born and a time to die, a time to plant and a time to uproot, a time to kill and a time to heal, a time to tear down and a time to build, a time to weep and a time to laugh, a time to mourn and a time to dance, a time to scatter stones and a time to gather them, a time to embrace and a time to refrain from embracing, a time to search and a time to give up, a time to keep and a time to throw away, a time to tear and a time to mend, a time to be silent and a time to speak, a time to love and a time to hate, a time for war and a time for peace.

Let's journey through some of the seasons we might be facing and the common scenarios that play out during these times.

The transition to a "winter" season can be tough. Perhaps we were living in the abundance of a summer season when the fruit was plentiful. But now God is saying it's time for a sabbatical. It's time to wait and rest. All our busyness comes to a halt. We can become weary here if not careful.

This sudden change of direction might catch us off guard if we are not listening closely to the Holy Spirit. We start questioning why. God may appear to be distant. Some other common ways to describe the "winter" season include the desert or the wilderness, like we felt after leaving Colorado. Things appear to be dying and dormant. We may feel lost. Galatians 5:24 says, "Those who belong to Christ Jesus have crucified the flesh with its passions and desires." We start to grapple with the reality that we are walking away from things we've loved and felt God called us to. This isn't selfish; each one of us needs to be filled up with the Holy Spirit to keep going! Rest is satisfying for our weary souls. God knows what we need more than we do. Resist the lies of the enemy here and wait on God for your next move. It's important to stand strong on a firm foundation during this time.

This season also requires us to find time for restoration, rebuilding, and strengthening our spiritual muscles for the next season. God wants to teach us new revelations and wisdom needed for the next season. This is a good opportunity to take inventory of what we are involved in and see what God wants us to continue or to lay down. Perhaps we are being prepared for a new direction on the other side of the winter season. If we don't slow down, we may not see the importance of resting. Don't drag it out by fighting against this season! Jesus got away to be with the Father, and if He made that a priority, don't you think we need to as well? This is a great season for reflecting and drawing closer to Him—or for what I like to describe as setting yourself apart. We accomplish this by waiting on God and being with Him. He empties us so that He can fill us up with more of Him.

After such a harsh season of dying to ourselves and waiting on God in our winter rest, we hopefully will begin to feel the warm wind of beautiful spring blowing in. Anticipation and expectation for new life and ideas are around the corner. Spring is all about growth! We are growing in unparalleled ways, and wisdom is poured out in abundance. We are walking in new freedoms. All of a sudden, anything is possible! We emerge from winter ready to birth new dreams and revelations that the Lord has placed in our hearts. It's time to take risks and step out of our previous refuge. We are springing forth into the new life He is giving us. Desires of the heart are downloaded, and new passions arise! We begin to dream again and see the possibility of new wine.

Matthew 9:17 says, "Neither do people pour new wine into old wineskins. If they do, the skins will burst; the wine will run out and the wineskins will be ruined. No, they pour new wine into new wineskins, and both are preserved." In this season, we must be ready to activate the new and put aside the old ways that no longer suffice. We don't forget what we went through, but we let what the fire forged in that season bring forth purpose. Perhaps we are okay with moving forward, even with an excitement for the new wine being poured into us. In the spring, we haven't seen the harvest yet, but we are seeing the beauty from ashes come alive.

In the summer season the harvest arrives! What was sown in the previous seasons, we will now reap. We are flourishing and feeling beyond blessed because of our relationship with Christ. The deep roots we grew from the intense trials, fiery ordeals, pain, and battles are now stable and secure enabling us to plant seeds in others and to glorify Christ! We have an abundance to pour out to the people God sets before us. We are busy working the harvest for the kingdom of God. Second Corinthians 9:10 states, "Now he who supplies seed to the sower and bread for food will also supply and increase your store of seed and will enlarge the harvest of your righteousness."

In this season, we are walking in spiritual wisdom, authority, and maturity. Having been refined by the fire, we are glowing with a radiant light! Glimpsing at the seeds sown in faith and the seeds being planted in others by us, we begin to perceive how Jesus walked us through suffering and used it for His glory. A partnership with Jesus emerges of helping others by sharing our stories of triumph over pain as we held onto Jesus's hand.

Each season should change us and grow us closer to Christ. We are continuously being made new. After our "summer harvest," the spiritual season of fall arrives. We may experience a "falling" away of some sort during this time, even a sense of loss. God starts to prune us, and we could start to wonder, "Why me, God?" This could mean we need to let go of something we didn't know we were exalting over our relationship with God. Sometimes we have to move away from those we love or go through a job loss. This is a "testing" season. We may need to pause and lay down sinful habits or break through the new or old bondages we've acquired. Transition is inevitable.

When we lose something, it can hurt even when we know it needs to go. Change is hard for most of us. But as we are learning, God is right there with us, comforting, holding, and providing for us in ways we never experienced before. He is waiting to bring restoration and healing to us. In the process of letting go, God is preparing us for something much better in the next season. As with all seasons, this one is temporary, and we need to be aware and embrace that after the surrendering and pruning, we will be changed. It may seem as if God is upset with us, but He is not. He disciplines those He loves. As Hebrews 12:6 says, "The Lord disciplines the one he loves, and he chastens everyone he accepts as his son." We are his children! He won't leave us as He found us.

God prunes us for new growth. In John 15:1–3 Jesus declares, "I am the true vine, and my Father is the gardener. He cuts off every branch in me that bears no fruit, while every branch that does bear fruit he prunes so that it will be even more fruitful. You are already clean because of the word I have spoken to you."

You will need to guard yourself and not allow the enemy to play with your mind and emotions during this season. To keep you in pain, he will try to shift your focus to what is being laid down or what you walked away from. He will attempt to make you believe that the bad circumstance you are in is too big for God. If it was something out of your control, the enemy will make you think it was all your fault. I encourage you to stand up against these lies! God says you are valuable and that He will never leave or forsake you. There is beauty in every season if you behold it for what it is and partake in the change that is happening.

As we walk through the hard seasons of our lives, I want you to remember each season eventually changes and brings us closer to God and serves His purposes in us. We must continue to press in and cling to Him and trust the process, so we are prepared for all He has for us. The process is about deepening our relationship with God, stripping us of harmful thoughts and actions, and burning off anything that does not please God or serve us well. All the trials, tribulations, and fiery ordeals are creating in us a light that shines brightly for others to see in this dark world.

How can we best navigate these different seasons? Here are some ideas:

- Ask God to help you steward the season well.
- Surrender the season to Him.
- Wait on Him for your next steps.
- Take communion and pray daily.
- Seek wise counsel from a trusted friend or someone at church.
- Spend time reading the Bible daily.
- Worship Him no matter how you feel.
- Pray His promises over your season.
- Rebuke the enemy.
- Fix your eyes on Jesus and not the distractions.

As we learn to recognize the different seasons—from fiery ordeals to bountiful harvests—we begin to see the fruit the hard work produces in our lives. We recognize what needs to be burned off so that we can not only shine the light of Jesus but also allow a beautiful incense to flow out of us, an "aroma of Christ". Join me as we continue our journey of trading our pain for beauty with Jesus, as we discuss the aroma of Christ and its power to draw others to Jesus as they spend time with us and sense Jesus in us.

Reflection

Where are you at in your painful season? Are you in the beginning or the middle, or do you sense it is coming to an end? What is God trying to teach you along the way so far? Remember that all seasons after a duration come to an end. Try to glean the lessons that God is laying before you even from the hard season you are going through.

CHAPTER 8

We Are the Sweet Aroma of Christ

"We are the aroma of Christ, not peddlers of a way of life, not sales people for a system of beliefs. We are those commissioned by God to transform the very air in which we live, not because of who we are but because of who He is."
~ Amanda Bible Williams

Did you know that everywhere we go we are giving off an aroma? Not the latest perfume you bought or essential oil but I'm referring to the essence or impression that we leave behind. After someone leaves your presence, do they sense there is something different about you? Or do they think, "Man, that person is a hot mess?"

A person's scent has a way of lingering with us. The Merriam-Webster dictionary states that an aroma is "a distinctive, pervasive, and usually pleasant smell or savory smell." It is subtle and has a pervasive quality or atmosphere of a particular type. From this definition, we know that an aroma is pleasant and pervasive!

That's a good thing because there are certain fragrances we want to be around and for it to linger. Personally, I can think of several aromas that I love. Chocolate chip cookies are definitely a favorite.

Oh, and I'm a pumpkin spice girl. The aroma drifting off a favorite candle makes the ambiance around me cozy and happy. Don't get me started on the smell of a coffee shop! The essence of these scents makes me want to linger in the presence of them. People can affect us in the same way.

Some people I know I just want to linger with. They make me feel loved, safe, and encouraged. Others I can't wait to exit their presence because of the negativity and bitterness they give off. I think you grasp the point: we give off aromas to those we encounter. Let's explore what the Bible has to say about the aroma we carry.

Second Corinthians 2:14–16 says, "But thanks be to God, who always leads us as captives in Christ's triumphal procession and uses us to spread the aroma of the knowledge of him everywhere. For we are to God the pleasing aroma of Christ among those who are being saved and those who are perishing. To the one we are an aroma that brings death; to the other, an aroma that brings life. And who is equal to such a task?"

As born-again believers we give off a pleasant, life-giving aroma to Christ and His children. But to those who reject Christ, the Bible says, it's the stench of death. This should move us to discern the hurt in them and want to love them toward Christ. How we live our life gives off an aroma to the world. How people perceive it, however, is different.

The scripture above says we are being led in a triumphal procession that God uses to spread His knowledge. A victory parade just like soldiers of long ago would have marched in! Check out the analogy I found online about this scripture at Got Questions:

> The apostle was speaking to the Corinthians about recent events in his ministry of evangelism. Despite all the difficulties and disappointments he'd faced while traveling from city to city

spreading the gospel, Paul is able to reflect on God's goodness with thanksgiving. The apostle then compared this ministry to evangelism to the triumphal military parades that occurred at that time in the Roman world.

Paul's metaphor would be readily understood by his audience, with the apostle and his co-laborers portrayed as victorious soldiers in a triumphal procession. During these Roman military parades, captives of war would be marched through the streets as garlands of flowers were carried and incense was burned to the gods. The aromatic perfumes wafted on the air as spectators and those in the procession breathed in their fragrance. At the parade's finale, many prisoners would be put to death. Thus, the aromas became sweet and life-giving to the victors, but they carried the stench of death to those who had been defeated.

In Paul's analogy, he separates humanity into two groups: those on the path of salvation and those on the road to destruction. The smell spread everywhere by the disciples, and it was the realization of God as victor. Christians who spread the gospel are members of God's victorious army led by Jesus Christ. Believers are like the essence or fragrance spread during the victory processions. Both the victors and those perishing give off an odor; however, it has a different meaning for the two groups. For the victorious army and its peoples, the aroma would relate to the joy of triumph. But for the prisoners of war, the fragrance would be associated with defeat, slavery, and death.[4]

Similarly, as we overcome the hard things in Jesus, as we proclaim victory over our circumstances through our partnership with Christ, our lives will send the message of joy and hope and life to others. If we choose to stay prisoners to our fear and suffering, it points people to hopelessness. How we overcome and endure our trials, sufferings, and afflictions has the potential to draw others to Christ. In the process of our old nature being burned off like incense, we begin to give off the sweet, attractive aroma to God and others.

I believe that when we have been touched by Jesus, we are never the same. Once this happens, you can never take in enough of His presence. You're compelled to talk about Him and think about Him in all you do. It's like when you buy a new outfit and can't wait to wear it to show your friends. Like a new outfit, we have been clothed in the garments of Jesus, so we want to show Him to everyone. This is the pleasant aroma we leave in the room. The people we were with should sense they have been with Jesus and be curious about where you got your new garments.

My question for you is what aroma are you leaving for someone who has been in your presence? Allowing Jesus to walk you through healing and trading your pain for His freedom leaves a welcoming fragrance to God and others. Jesus wants to radically transform you and breathe life into your dry bones. He wants others to notice your healing so that they have hope too. Jesus wants the essence of *His*

---

4   "What Does It Mean That Christians Are the Aroma of Christ?" GotQuestions. org, accessed March 21, 2024, https://www.gotquestions.org/aroma-of-Christ. html.

presence to linger in a room and on a person after they leave your presence.

You want to know how to give off the sweet aroma of Christ? There are several ways, but a predominant way is prayer. The more time we spend with Jesus in His presence, in prayer, and re-wallpapering our minds with His Word, the more strongly the aroma of Christ will be on us.

As we pray, our prayers send up a sweet aroma to Jesus! The more time we spend on the things of Jesus, the more His very DNA becomes ours. We are born again, remember? We must learn to live in this new birth. Our eyes must open to His Spirit in us. When we spend time in prayer, this gives off the pleasing aroma God is looking for. In Leviticus we learn how the priests burned incense on the golden altar, and this represented the prayers of the people!

In fact, Revelation 5:8 describes golden bowls of incense, which are the prayers of the saints. "But I am not a saint," you might be thinking. Guess what? Acts 9:32 (ESV) says, "Now as Peter went here and there among them all, he came down also to the saints who lived at Lydda." This is one of many scriptures that call the people of God "saints," meaning set apart for God. We are called saints by God! This includes you and me!

What are some kinds of prayers we can partner with Jesus in? Prayers asking for the salvation of unbelievers, overcoming unforgiveness, seeking wisdom and revelation, encountering His peace and presence, interceding for others, making petitions and supplications, praising Him, and asking for His kingdom and will to be done, and expressing thankfulness, to name a few. We can pray about anything!

Our prayers allow Jesus to lead us well and keep us in close relationship with Him. Prayer is submitting our will to His will. Not only do we begin to detect Him working in our lives, but others will see Him working in and changing us too. Second Corinthians 2:14

(NLT) states, "But thank God! He has made us his captives and continues to lead us along in Christ's triumphal procession. Now he uses us to spread the knowledge of Christ everywhere, like a sweet perfume."

Our prayers matter. How we live matters. Others are watching us, and when we live prayerful lives for Christ and let Him lead us, this spreads the knowledge of Him for others to catch hold of. Others behold the power of God leading us through our prayers. It becomes a sweet aroma when our prayers are answered, giving hope to others. This is how we partner with Jesus to change the outcomes here on earth and for His will to be done.

In addition to prayer, repentance is another way we exude the sweet aroma of Christ—first with Jesus and then we can extend or seek forgiveness with others in our life.

The woman at the well did precisely this. In John 4, we learn about a Samaritan woman whose life was changed after an encounter with Jesus. Afterward, she gave off the sweet smell of Jesus instead of the stench of an adulteress. She received forgiveness for her sins from the Savior and many in her town believed in Jesus because of her testimony. In fact, she ran through her village saying, "He told me everything I ever did!" (John 4:39). She couldn't keep quiet about her encounter. This testimony caused others to check out Jesus for themselves. Her aroma was too sweet to ignore. She carried the essence of God all over her town. Like her story, repentance is our foundation of walking with Jesus.

To really understand the aroma of Christ, we need to look back at the sacrifices described in the Old Testament. Here is where we will find the main way and reason for attaining this aroma for ourselves. These sacrifices, or burnt offerings as they were called, for the people's sins gave off a pleasing aroma to God, and when He encountered the scent, He would be satisfied with their sacrifice to atone for their sins. Before Jesus walked the earth, God's chosen people, the Israelites, received the law or commandments to live by. These commandments housed the guidelines, laws, and rules for them to live as a people set apart for God as a holy people. God contained them in these boundaries. These laws protected them and kept them living their best life, so to speak, until Jesus came and died on the cross for all of mankind.

The Hebrew word used for "burnt offering" means to ascend or literally go up in smoke. According to Leviticus 1:9 this is "an aroma pleasing to the Lord." This sacrifice atoned for the people's sins and made things right between them and God. God had very specific instructions on how these sacrifices needed to be completed. The animal that would be sacrificed had to have no defect or blemish on it. All of this laid the foundation for the ultimate sacrifice, Jesus dying on the cross for the sins of mankind. All of this in the Old Testament pointed to Jesus!

God freely gave this gift to us. If we receive the gift, acknowledge our sins, repent for them, and enter a relationship with Jesus, we become in right standing with God. Jesus's sacrifice is the final pleasing aroma for the atonement of sin. Living in repentance and knowledge of our need for God becomes a delightful scent to God; then it draws others to the fragrance as well.

Numbers 15:3 tells us it's what the people offered that became the pleasing aroma to the Lord. On the cross, Jesus was the offering. His sacrifice became a pleasing aroma. Only Jesus can cleanse us and create in us pure hearts. Offering ourselves to God, broken before Him in a way that only He can mend, allows us to be changed and to carry Jesus's essence in us. Psalm 51:17 says, "My sacrifice, O God, is a broken spirit; a broken and contrite heart you, God, will not despise." God loves for us to abide in Him in a posture of humility and surrender, offering ourselves to Him.

Only then will our essence become Christ Himself. Jesus is the final sacrifice, but because He lives in us, through the Holy Spirit, we carry this fragrance. Accepting Jesus's gift of salvation is the primary way we give off the aroma of Christ. Our relationship with Him through prayer and our repentance then follows.

What are some other ways we can give off the aroma of Christ? One way is by understanding that the Holy Spirit lives in us, giving us the power to overcome our sin natures. As we trade our sins, habits, and hurts for God's ways, we begin to give off a pleasing aroma to God and others.

Another way is presenting our bodies as a living sacrifice. Romans 12:1 says, "Therefore, I urge you, brothers and sisters, in view of God's mercy, to offer your bodies as a living sacrifice I appeal to you therefore, brothers, by the mercies of God, to present your bodies as a living sacrifice, holy and pleasing to God-this is your true and proper worship." Again, how we live matters to God. Jesus declares we were bought with a price. We didn't pay the price but once we receive that gift, we need to live for Him in order to spread the aroma to others.

Paul, who wrote the book of Corinthians, knew better than anyone how to lay his life down for Christ. In 1 Corinthians 6:20 Paul says, "you were bought at a price. Therefore honor God with your bodies." Paul was first known for persecuting Christians, and then in a dramatic turn of events he became a disciple of Jesus. Jesus turned his life upside down. In turn, Paul laid his entire life down for the cause of Jesus. In Philippians 1:12–14, Paul writes, "Now I want you to know, brothers and sisters, that what has happened to me has actually served to advance the gospel. As a result, it has become clear throughout the whole palace guard and to everyone else that I am in chains for Christ. And because of my chains, most of the brothers and sisters have become confident in the Lord and dare all the more to proclaim the gospel without fear." Paul surrendered everything, and his aroma built the people's confidence to be bold for the cause!

Ultimately, carrying this aroma comes from a sacrifice on our own part. We lay our lives down for Jesus. Our desires. Our bodies. Our pain and suffering. Our fears. We must seek healing through Jesus so He can make us whole. Then, overflowing with His presence, we can begin to give off His aroma. The purpose of giving off His aroma: to draw others to Him in love.

When we walk in love toward others, even to those who don't necessarily deserve it, the aroma of Christ is released from us. Ephesians 5:2 says, "and walk in the way of love, just as Christ loved us and gave himself up for us as a fragrant offering and sacrifice to God." Walking in love even when it's hard puts God front and center in our lives, and people will take notice. This doesn't mean we don't respond to hurt or danger; it only means that when we respond with a loving heart, it lets God move in that person. We can walk away "well" and leave the fragrance of Christ with that person even if it means we no longer have relationship with them. This is how we live in a place of loving God and loving others well. It's who He called us to be. Fiery ordeals burn off what's not needed and allow what's left to flourish into a beautiful, attractive aroma.

I was completely emptied out when I lost Brennen. I was a shell. After a complete surrendering to God of what was left of me, the change started to take place. This was the perfect place for Jesus to fill me back up with His presence—His sweet aroma—so that I could pour it out to others. When we die to ourselves, as Paul describes, the Holy Spirit can begin to freely move through us for the benefit of others and to bring about God's kingdom.

Kathryn Kuhlman was an evangelist who lived from 1907 to 1976 and was known for her healing services. She lived a life that gave off the aroma of Christ. Like Paul, she knew that the secret to being a pleasing aroma for Jesus was dying to ourselves. She said, "All He needs is someone who will die, and when I died, He came in. I was baptized. I was filled with the Spirit. I spoke in an unknown tongue as He took every part of me. In that moment, I surrendered unto Him all there was of me, everything. Everything. Then, for the first time I realized what it meant to have power."

When we walk through our trials and give them to God, others can pick up on the aroma of Christ in us. Why? Because He takes the ingredients of our heartache and hurt and turns them into a beautiful aroma of His goodness. This in turn draws others to the Father's love. They want what we have, which is Jesus. They recognize there is something different about us. They like the aroma that was left lingering from our presence: Jesus in us!

How do we know what aroma we are leaving behind to others? First, we can see how others respond to spending time with us. What are they saying after hanging out with us? What are people asking us? Do they say things like, "I feel like Jesus was speaking right to me when you shared your story," or "What you said was exactly what I needed to hear." I've left conversations when the other person says, "I see Jesus in you." We should leave others thinking about Jesus. We should let them know that Jesus is inviting them into so much more than their own stories of heartache.

The key to remember is that our lives lived for Jesus are not one and done. It's daily prayer time, repenting, surrendering, and figuring out how to love others. There will be seasons of us going deeper and deeper as we follow Jesus. As we hold onto His hand, He will be with us every step of the way. We will look back at the things we laid down and see how He brought beauty from the hard places. As we continue to rely on Him and stay in faith, we will learn that He doesn't leave us and our foundation in Him gets stronger and steadier every day. Then when the storms of life hit, we won't be as shaken. We will remember the last storm so when the next one hits, we know the power of God will get us through it.

As we close this chapter and venture into the next, we will be looking at the book of Job. We can't talk about suffering and ignore the book of Job in the Bible. There is much to learn.

Reflection

In the process of thinking about the painful memories you have gone through, take time to reflect on what aroma you are giving off to others. Trust me, I know how hard life can be. But with Jesus, you can be an overcomer. Does your life give off the fragrance of hope, healing, forgiveness, peace, and freedom? Or does your life give off the aroma of bitterness, hatred, and unforgiveness? If it's the latter, Jesus wants to trade that aroma for one only He can give you. Immersing yourself in prayer, God's Word, community with other believers, and reliance on Jesus is where you will begin to give off the aroma of Christ to others. His healing power is in you.

CHAPTER 9

Lessons from Job

*"Whenever God restores something, He restores
it to a place greater than it was before."*
~ Bill Johnson

Tucked away in the Old Testament is the book of Job. Job is known for his journey through immense loss and suffering. There are many lessons to be gleaned from this book that can help us navigate our own stories as well as teach us how to help others in theirs.

At first glance this book can really mess with our theology. It can be hard to follow if it's your first time reading it. But as we walk through trials and suffering, studying Job's story gives us new perspectives in dealing with it. The opening scene is very interesting, so let's start there:

> There was a man in the land of Uz whose
> name was Job, and that man was blameless and
> upright, one who feared God and turned away
> from evil. There were born to him seven sons
> and three daughters. He possessed 7,000 sheep,
> 3,000 camels, 500 yoke of oxen, and 500 female

donkeys, and very many servants, so that this man was the greatest of all the people of the east. His sons used to go and hold a feast in the house of each one on his day, and they would send and invite their three sisters to eat and drink with them. And when the days of the feast had run their course, Job would send and consecrate them, and he would rise early in the morning and offer burnt offerings according to the number of them all. For Job said, "It may be that my children have sinned, and cursed God in their hearts." Thus Job did continually.

Now there was a day when the sons of God came to present themselves before the LORD, and Satan also came among them. The LORD said to Satan, "From where have you come?" Satan answered the LORD and said, "From going to and fro on the earth, and from walking up and down on it." And the LORD said to Satan, "Have you considered my servant Job, that there is none like him on the earth, a blameless and upright man, who fears God and turns away from evil?" Then Satan answered the LORD and said, "Does Job fear God for no reason? Have you not put a hedge around him and his house and all that he has on every side? You have blessed the work of his hands, and his possessions have increased in the land. But stretch out your hand and touch all that he has, and he will curse you to your face." And the LORD said to Satan, "Behold, all that he has is in your hand. Only against him do not stretch out your hand." So Satan went out from the presence of the LORD.

Now there was a day when his sons and daughters were eating and drinking wine in their oldest brother's house, and there came a messenger to Job and said, "The oxen were plowing and the donkeys feeding beside them, and the Sabeans fell upon them and took them and struck down the servants with the edge of the sword, and I alone have escaped to tell you." While he was yet speaking, there came another and said, "The fire of God fell from heaven and burned up the sheep and the servants and consumed them, and I alone have escaped to tell you." While he was yet speaking, there came another and said, "The Chaldeans formed three groups and made a raid on the camels and took them and struck down the servants with the edge of the sword, and I alone have escaped to tell you." While he was yet speaking, there came another and said, "Your sons and daughters were eating and drinking wine in their oldest brother's house, and behold, a great wind came across the wilderness and struck the four corners of the house, and it fell upon the young people, and they are dead, and I alone have escaped to tell you."

Then Job arose and tore his robe and shaved his head and fell on the ground and worshiped. And he said, "Naked I came from my mother's womb, and naked shall I return. The LORD gave, and the LORD has taken away; blessed be the name of the LORD." In all this Job did not sin or charge God with wrong. (Job 1:1–22 ESV)

Let's take in what we can learn from this chapter of Job. First, Job is said to be blameless and upright in God's sight. Job has not only feared God and turned away from evil, but he has even offered sacrifices in case his children forgot to repent for anything. Job followed God's heart and commands. This shows that sometimes bad things can happen to righteous people. God's not causing the bad things; the reality is, we live in a fallen world and Satan is always going to and fro trying to kill, steal, and destroy our lives. And don't forget we have free will.

As we read, the scene shifts from Job's blessed life to a courtroom of heaven. Satan approaches the throne room of God and must give an answer to what he has been up to. To our surprise, God asks Satan if he's considered his servant Job in his wanderings on the earth.

Wait, what? I don't know about you, but the first time I ever read that, it blew my mind. First of all, Satan is in the throne room, and he approaches God, and second of all, God asks him if he has considered messing with Job. At first glance I'm not sure if that question makes me upset with God or if I find comfort in knowing that even Satan is limited.

We are told that Job has a hedge of protection around him and all that belongs to him. Satan cannot just do whatever he wants to Job— boundaries exist. Satan must get permission to test him. Nothing can take place in our lives that God does not know about. The Scriptures point to the sovereignty of God. As a believer, knowing that God is in control should bring us peace. The blood of Jesus covers us and protects us. If we are not believers, however, the hedge of protection is not around us. Ultimately, though, if we *are* abiding in Jesus, we can find comfort in knowing Satan cannot do whatever he wants to us.

Let that sink in. If Satan approaches God and obtains permission to test us, we can trust that God works for the good of those who love Him, who have been called according to His purposes (see Romans 8:28). God sees the bigger picture, knows our hearts, and is in control of the outcome.

We can trust God's bigger purpose for what is going on in our lives. God is not the author of bad things happening, but He is the master at working in these hard circumstances to bring about eternal purposes, which are far more important than our temporary lives here. So what happens to Job? He loses everything. What can we learn from Job and how does his response help us in our seasons of trials, loss and suffering? Let's categorize it by the conversations Job has with himself, his friends, and ultimately God.

After his loss, Job goes through the process we all must go through. A process of trying to make sense of it all. Our emotions can be all over the place. Job goes through the most common hardships we all encounter: health battles, financial difficulties, and loss of loved ones. Job's wife even becomes a source of contention when she says to Job in Job 2:9–10, "'Are you still maintaining your integrity? Curse God and die!' He replied, 'You are talking like a foolish woman. Shall we accept good from God, and not trouble?' In all this, Job did not sin in what he said." How often does the enemy attack us when we are down? Everything in Job's world is turned upside down; it would seem fair for him to be angry with God.

However, that's why it's important to know God's Word so we know the truth. If we stay in prayer, it will keep us from being trapped by the enemy's lies or someone else's wrong advice. It's helpful to have wise counsel from someone full of the Holy Spirit to pray with us and encourage us during hard times, so we are not left alone to our thoughts and emotions.

In the second part, in walks Job's three friends to comfort him. Their names are Eliphaz, Bildad, and Zophar. Let's read about them in Job 2:11–13 (ESV):

> Now when Job's three friends heard of all this evil that had come upon him, they came each from his own place, Eliphaz the Temanite, Bildad the Shuhite, and Zophar the Naamathite. They made an appointment together to come to show him sympathy and comfort him. And when they saw him from a distance, they did not recognize him. And they raised their voices and wept, and they tore their robes and sprinkled dust on their heads toward heaven. And they sat with him on the ground seven days and seven nights, and no one spoke a word to him, for they saw that his suffering was very great.

So far, so good, right? All of us can learn a thing or two from Job's friends about how to help others. They come to sit with Job and just be with him. They want to bring sympathy and comfort. Where it goes wrong for them and often does for us is they start trying to figure out the motives, the whys, and they really want to have an answer for Job, but they don't. Like them, it makes us feel better to offer advice, but sometimes we don't know the whole story. We want to help, but we often need to let Jesus work things out in others' lives so they can come to their own healing place and growth.

Of course, we can pray for them, offer scriptural encouragement, listen to them, lead them to Jesus. But we should avoid trying to fix someone. Only Jesus has the power to do that. In the worst places, Jesus really comes through, and it's important we learn to lean into

Him in our pain. Having everything stripped away, where all we have is Jesus, is a safe place to land.

There have been times I have assumed I understood why something was happening to someone. I have also learned, when I'm walking through difficult seasons, others may act like they have all the answers to my problems, but it's not always helpful.

It's when I sat with Jesus, Him and me alone, in these difficult places, that I could hear His voice louder than everyone else's. While we are waiting on God, it can often feel like others are judging our decisions. It can be prideful or arrogant on our part, when we think we have it all figured out as to why someone is going through difficult times, without considering God in the equation.

We may have some obvious answers, but we don't always have the whole story. Only God sees the bigger picture. We want so badly to understand, but as we learn from the book of Job, that's not always the case. Job's friends are convinced that he's carried hidden sin or that he did something wrong to be in this predicament. They even misrepresent God.

This gives us the scandalous story, right? The gossip and juicy details we hope for. This kind of thinking also makes us feel better about ourselves, telling ourselves we would never do that or act like that or find ourselves in that situation.

I remember finding ways to feel guilty about Brennen's death—as if somehow I could have stopped it. That was not even realistic in his situation, being born with a heart defect. That was not my fault, nor God's fault. In that situation, it was a consequence of living in a world tainted by sin and imperfection. Babies can be born with physical problems. I didn't need to listen to the accusations of the enemy.

I was not walking with God at the time Brennen died. Satan appeared to have free range to do what he wanted. I did not have God's hedge of protection. Thankfully, though, through it all, God waited for me to turn to Him. It's important to remember that Job was found blameless—in right standing with God—and he was living with God's hedge of protection. Satan couldn't just do whatever he wanted. He had to have permission. This can be hard to understand, but when we walk with God, what the enemy means for harm God uses for growth.

Job's friends' remarks do not help in the long run. Their words are hurtful and provide no relief. It's best if we process our hurts with Jesus, the only true healer. Job's thoughts were something he had to sift through with God. His friends only brought confusion. God knew Job as blameless; God saw Job's heart and motives. We can't automatically assign motive like Job's friends—that's a secret place that only God perceives.

The part we can take from Job's friends is to love and support those who are struggling and leave the accusations at the door. Job was already asking himself the same things they were asking him. His friends became self-righteous, something we can all be prone to do. Ouch!

We need to make sure, when our lives seem to be going well and others' lives are not, that we do not think it's because we are better than they are. Pride always comes before the fall. Jesus clearly states in John 9:3, "'Neither this man nor his parents sinned,' said Jesus, 'but this happened so that the works of God might be displayed in him.'" God has a way of working things out so that He gets the glory.

God has purposes and outcomes that we can't fathom. Like I've mentioned, it's a process we must walk through. Remember, the key is not to remain stuck in these unhealthy places but to keep looking to God, just like Job did. Don't skip out on this process of healing with Jesus! There's something beautiful about pouring out our souls at His feet while holding onto His hand.

In addition to his friends, Job had conversations with God throughout his grieving process. Job asked the "why me?" question a lot! And he was met with God's silence. He had to wrestle with God about all he was going through and feeling. This is where the wrestling takes place for us too—in the hard conversations with God.

Job eventually came to a place of surrender to God in a greater measure. Just like we must do, Job settled that he didn't have control. He discovered that God was sovereign and faithful despite what he was going through. Similarly, we must trust that God has our best interest in mind. This is how our relationship with God is forged with deep roots. This is where true healing happens.

This didn't happen for me at first; there's a process and journey to surrendering. Staying close to Jesus through the hard times allows Him to open a way to restoration in us and to our situations. Sometimes, like Job, we don't get the "why did it happen?" answered. But we take hold of Jesus, and that is more than enough. That is better than the answer. I hope you see what we are receiving in exchange for our pain—the presence of Jesus—and that changes everything. We get to be in relationship with the King of Kings! We get to walk in intimacy with the Holy Spirit in us.

How do we walk like Job through our pain and loss? We follow Job's lead by pouring out our soul at the feet of Jesus. We can ask all the questions and cry as much as we need to with Jesus. He is the only comforter that provides lasting benefits. One of my favorite scriptures is Psalm 126:5: "Those who sow with tears will reap with songs of joy." Sowing our tears at the feet of Jesus in surrender will ultimately reap joy for us—we obtain a completely different outcome than what was expected. As people say, "Only God."

As I learned to surrender my grief and pain to Jesus and trust Him with the outcome, He began to show me my true inheritance in Him. This world is only temporary, and He came to seek and save what has been lost, including me and my family! This is what we gain.

First Peter 1:4 tells us that we have been born again into an inheritance that can never perish, spoil, or fade. It's kept in heaven for us, and we have the Holy Spirit in us as a down payment! Nothing can taint Jesus Christ and His Word. It's imperishable. When we understand the value of our inheritance and what awaits us, we can endure whatever comes our way. As 2 Corinthians 4:17 says, "For our light and momentary troubles are achieving for us an eternal glory that far outweighs them all."

Jesus invites us into His perfect plan. God knows that whatever we go through in this life with Jesus is nothing compared to all of eternity without Him. He gives us opportunities in our afflictions to draw closer to Him and choose Him. God is moving toward ultimate vindication and restoration for all who are lost due to the fall in the garden of Eden.

We can experience victory here on earth in our painful circumstances, but we are also moving toward a culmination of all things being made right again. We must see like Jesus does—from a kingdom mind-set. Everything in this world is fading fast. We are building toward an eternal kingdom with Jesus forever. As we stay close to Jesus and allow Him to shape us, empty us, and mold us for eternity, we begin to grasp what we are laying down here for our inheritance in heaven.

God is in the business of restoration. The word *restoration* according to the Merriam-Webster Dictionary online means "an act of restoring or the condition of being restored such as: a bringing back to a former position or condition." Mankind and the earth will not only be made new, but they will be better than before!

Think about Job—he lost everything! Yet he never walked away from God, and God brought restoration. Job kept his faith and fear of God. This is our goal as well.

Imagine the wisdom and depth of relationship and intimacy with God that Job lived with after walking through that process. Job 42:10–17 says,

After Job had prayed for his friends, the Lord restored his fortunes and gave him twice as much as he had before. All his brothers and sisters and everyone who had known him before came and ate with him in his house. They comforted and consoled him over all the trouble the Lord had brought on him, and each one gave him a piece of silver and a gold ring.

The Lord blessed the latter part of Job's life more than the former part. He had fourteen thousand sheep, six thousand camels, a thousand yoke of oxen and a thousand donkeys. And he also had seven sons and three daughters. The first daughter he named Jemimah, the second Keziah and the third Keren-Happuch. Nowhere in all the land were there found women as beautiful as Job's daughters, and their father granted them an inheritance along with their brothers.

After this, Job lived a hundred and forty years; he saw his children and their children to the fourth generation. And so Job died, an old man and full of years.

Did you notice that Job's restoration came after he prayed for his friends? That's interesting to note. To move forward, Job extended forgiveness to his friends, and they asked God for forgiveness for misrepresenting Him. The enemy tried so hard to ensnare Job in a spirit of offense. But through his challenges, Job surrendered to God. Job never cursed God like the devil said he would. This lays a foundation for us to emphasize how important forgiveness is to God.

After Job wrestles through the process of loss and despair with God—God later fully restores everything Job has lost, and Job ends up changed for the better—He gets to know God personally. He gains more than just head knowledge about God. He doesn't just follow a list of religious rules of dos and don'ts. Job encounters the sovereignty of God as well as God's character and heart. He has gained a much better eternal perspective from what he walked through.

As I reflect on losing Brennen, I can see all that God restored. His blessings are limitless. He gave me two more boys and a family who loves Jesus. He gave me unshakable faith and love for Him. He gave me peace and hope and security. He has nothing but goodness and love for me. He gave me a future and a hope that I couldn't fathom at the time. The best part is He gave me His presence. What more could I ask for?

The question is, do you want the same gifts—to grasp the truth, freedom, and restoration that only Jesus can offer? Let's fix our eyes on God, like Job did, and trust God will bring restoration out of our loss too. Let's have childlike faith in Him. Just like kids who trust their parents, who see the bigger picture and understand what their children can't perceive. Let's not forget that it is God who Job poured out his heart to—the good, the bad, and the ugly.

We are going to address one of the greatest benefits of walking through pain with Jesus in the next chapter: how we go from prodigals looking for a home to children of God with an eternal home built on an unshakable foundation. We touched on our inheritance in this chapter, but let's next take a closer look at our eternal inheritance in Jesus that is beyond our wildest imaginations.

Reflection

I encourage you to read the entire chapter of Job for yourself and see what God might want to say to you. As you read, ask the Holy Spirit to give you revelation about your own story of pain. What do you find surprising in the book of Job, and what do you find comforting? In what ways might God be wanting to bring restoration to your situation?

CHAPTER 10

Prodigal's Return

"Faith in Christ doesn't mean you won't suffer.
Instead it offers you the gift that when you
suffer you get to be more like Christ."
~ Unknown

Have you ever rented a house or apartment before? I have, and while I believe you can make any house a home by who and what is inside, there is something beautiful about owning your own place; it is freedom and security. Your own space to do whatever you want with the property—change the color of the paint on the walls, add on a room, or even tear down a wall. Home ownership feels good because we get to make something our own.

My husband and I purchased our first house the year Brennen was born. The excitement of building a house was indescribable. Getting to choose the flooring, kitchen counters, cabinets, and neighborhood is marvelous because we got to prepare the perfect place for ourselves—not just make do in a rental that had been built based on someone else's ideal residence.

Jesus says He is preparing a place for us. Our very own home. Can you imagine what kind of accommodation this will be? John 14:1–4 says, "Do not let your hearts be troubled. You believe in God;

believe also in me. My Father's house has many rooms; if that were not so, would I have told you that I am going there to prepare a place for you? And if I go and prepare a place for you, I will come back and take you to be with me so that you also may be where I am. You know the way to the place where I am going."

This place is a permanent home that we get to live in for all eternity. This home is part of the incredible legacy as a child of God. We are no longer orphans but adopted into God's kingdom. Ephesians 1:5 (NLT) says, "God decided in advance to adopt us into his own family by bringing us to himself through Jesus Christ."

Moving from being a prodigal to a child of God means we no longer have to wander around, but instead, we have a home with deep roots and a lasting foundation. One with the perfect paint color and accommodations designed for each of us. Jesus can't wait for His children to be with Him forever in heaven. He invites us to begin the journey here on earth, our temporary living space. We are only passing through. Like a rented house, it's not our permanent home. Just a rented place to live until we receive our birthright in heaven.

I often think about Jesus going to the cross. Jesus willingly did this to save His children. He wishes none of us to perish (see 2 Peter 3:9). This is His heart. I also think about the power that raised Him from the dead and defeated hell. That same power is available to us because of the Holy Spirit in us. God put His spirit, power, and authority in us. All looked grim the moment Jesus died. However, Jesus rose from the grave as an overcomer and conqueror. Without the death and burial there would be no resurrection.

I believe this same concept applies to our individual lives as well. Part of the purpose in suffering is that it allows us to experience God's mercy and grace. Suffering often brings His lost children straight into His arms, which in turn, allows us to experience God's heart and love for us. It helps us draw our strength from God and not the temporal circumstances we face.

We can't lose sight of the fact that we live in a fallen world and bad things happen. Or that the enemy is meddling in our lives. The kingdom of darkness has an agenda, and it's to kill, steal, and destroy. John 10:10 states, "The thief comes only to steal and kill and destroy; I have come that they may have life and have it to the full." The devil is always prowling around looking for ways to trap us. We must stay on guard.

I believe there are several factors at play in any given situation: God's sovereignty, people's free will, and the devil's snares. Where the devil wants to destroy us, God wants us to have a future. When Jesus died on the cross, He made a public example of the kingdom of darkness. It became disarmed by the work of the cross. Jesus gave us authority in His name to drive out the enemy and take back territory that was stolen in our lives. We must exercise this authority over the enemy's schemes. Colossians 2:15 says, "And having disarmed the powers and authorities, he made a public spectacle of them, triumphing over them by the cross."

How do we exercise this authority? The Bible says the Word of God is living and active! We must decree and declare His Word over our situations. Take scripture and pray them out over our circumstances. Exalt God above it all and invite Him into our lives. Trust that He holds our heartache in His capable hands and will see us through to the other side. Wait on Him to do what only He can do. Shut the door in the enemy's face and rebuke him from your life and situation. Cancel his weapons and assignments by declaring God's truths and will over your life.

God says He turns our ashes into beauty and that He is working out all things for those who love Him. How can we trust that God is working out all things for our good? Here is how this works. We have established we are going to suffer in this fallen world. We can suffer to suffer, or we can submit to the lordship of Jesus Christ, and our suffering will be turned into something beautiful. Only in Jesus can this happen.

When Jesus died on the cross, it appeared all was lost. Oh, the agony, defeat, despair, and devastation his friends and family experienced. Little did they understand that in three days Jesus was going to resurrect from the grave. What appeared to be the worst case turned out to be the best-case scenario. Only the power of God can do that! Jesus does that for us too.

Jesus enters our devastating circumstances and brings something good out of them. When we encounter the presence of God, the awful experience we endured fades in comparison to His promises and love. Beauty and goodness can now be seen, despite the loss, suffering, pain, or hurt. Jesus's presence and goodness are stunning.

When my son passed away, I encountered the life-giving power of Jesus, and it changed my life and my family's life. The Holy Spirit gave me everything I needed to move on in this world, knowing Jesus held Brennen and me. Remember I said I heard the Holy Spirit say to me, "Heather, this is about you coming back to me." The beauty for my ashes was a homecoming to my heavenly Father. Luke 15 teaches us a parable about a shepherd with a hundred sheep. One of the sheep goes missing, and what does the shepherd do? Does he say, "Oh well, I still have ninety-nine sheep." No! He goes and finds the lost one. Then he rejoices when he finds the sheep. This is exactly what Jesus did for you and me. Jesus found me that day in that hospital room and said, "It's time to come back home. Let me pick you up and carry you back."

I often hear the statement "I can't believe in a God who would allow that to happen." But the way I see it is this tragedy happened because of the fallen world I live in. God didn't stop it, but He did reach down and offer Himself to me in it. Jesus became my lifeline. He said, "I'm sorry this is what happened, but my mercy and grace will carry you through this if you let me."

On the night Brennen passed away, as I previously shared, when I laid down on my bed lost in the shock of the moment, I encountered a supernatural presence that took over my body. I felt the presence of Jesus wash over me, and I could not move or talk. I was paralyzed with the weight of God's glory on me. I made out an outline of Brennen and as it passed through my mind I had a feeling that he was okay, he was with Jesus, and that Jesus was with me. This was that familiar weight of God I experienced as a little girl too.

Jesus revealed His presence to me on more than one occasion as a young girl. It was the weight of His glory. My body would become so heavy I couldn't move, and I would feel His incredible presence and hear in my spirit that He is my God. God is so very real. So very familiar. When I experienced His presence that night, I knew without a shadow of doubt God was with me. Jesus knew me and I knew Him, and He reminded me He holds it all in His hands. I could trust Him, and I invited Him in.

Jesus saved me from my sin and gave me insight, understanding, purpose, and destiny. I could grasp the bigger purpose. Could God have saved Brennen and healed him? Absolutely, but the bigger picture is if that would have happened, I may not have turned to God and would have spent all of eternity in hell forever separated from my Father. Jesus understood my suffering would turn me back to Him, and now my eternal well-being is secure in Him along with that of my family, because this event affected us all.

God gets the ultimate victory. Satan thought he could destroy me, but God spoke otherwise. I love this scripture: "For our light and momentary troubles are achieving for us an eternal glory that far outweighs them all. So we fix our eyes not on what is seen, but on what is unseen, since what is seen is temporary, but what is unseen is eternal" (2 Corinthians 4:17–18). Life is short, but eternity is forever.

So my light and momentary troubles on earth—no matter how traumatic—processed in Christ, are for such a small moment when compared to all eternity with God. In our moments of suffering Christ can turn our hearts back to Him.

God knows that suffering brings us to a crossroads. People often run to Him in these times—commonly for the first time. Or, as in my case, people are sometimes brought back to Him. The Bible tells the parable of the lost son, or the prodigal son. This is everyone's story at some point in their life.

Let's take a moment to read this parable in Luke 15:11–24:

> Jesus continued: "There was a man who had two sons. The younger one said to his father, 'Father, give me my share of the estate.' So he divided his property between them."

> "Not long after that, the younger son got together all he had, set off for a distant country and there squandered his wealth in wild living. After he had spent everything, there was a severe famine in that whole county, and he began to be in need. So he went and hired himself out to a citizen of that country, who sent him to his fields to feed pigs. He longed to fill his stomach with the pods that the pigs were eating, but no one gave him anything."

> "When he came to his senses, he said, 'How many of my father's hired servants have food to spare, and here I am starving to death! I will set out and go back to my father and say to him: Father, I have sinned against heaven and against you. I am no longer worthy to be called your

son; make me like one of your hired servants. So he got up and went to his father."

"But while he was still a long way off, the father saw him and was filled with compassion for him; he ran to his son, threw his arms around him and kissed him. The son said to to him, 'Father, I have sinned against heaven and you. I am no longer worthy to be called your son.'"

"But the father said to his servants, 'Quick! Bring the best robe and put it on him. Put a ring on his finger and sandals on his feet. Bring the fattened calf and kill it. Let's have a feast and celebrate. For this son of mine was dead and is alive again; he was lost and is found.' So they began to celebrate."

This story resonated with me when my son passed away. God didn't punish me for not walking with Him all those years. He welcomed me back with open arms in the condition I showed up in. All of heaven rejoiced. Jesus began preparing my inheritance in heaven with Him.

This parable is about a loving father—who represents our Father God—welcoming his lost son back—in my case, His daughter. Jesus died for our sins so that we all can come back to the Father. God is a good Father and wishes none of His children to perish. I was lost, but then I became found in Him. I had gone astray, and yet my Father waited on my return, knowing that I would make a mess out of my life without Him. I was dead without Jesus. Just like the prodigal's father, He offers so much compassion to us when we return to Him.

God celebrates when we return home to Him, too—where we have always belonged. Jesus loves us, He is for us, He lavishes immense gifts on us, and He paid the ultimate price by shedding His blood for our sin. God loves us more than we will ever understand this side of heaven. As we begin to perceive His heart behind everything written in His Word and what He did for us, we get a glimpse of this tremendous love.

Jesus throws us a lifeline to hang onto, which is His presence, the Holy Spirit. We are then invited into a beautiful inheritance that lasts all of eternity. As Ephesians 1:11 says, "In him we were also chosen, having been predestined according to the plan of him who works out everything in conformity with the purpose of his will."

Our birthright will be fully realized in heaven when we go from our temporal, rented home to our permanent, eternal home. We will be with Jesus forever. Our reward is our inheritance with Him according to Colossians 3:24. Nothing can take away the promises of God from us as His children unless we choose to disown God ourselves. We can walk through the hard things in this life with the power of the Holy Spirit in us because we know it's temporary and our inheritance is waiting for us in heaven—reserved for us, unspoiled, and not perishable. Glory awaits us, and it spurs us on in Jesus.

Revelation 21 paints a beautiful picture of what is coming, the ultimate restoration of all things:

> Then I saw "a new heaven and a new earth," for the first heaven and the first earth had passed away, and there was no longer any sea. I saw the Holy City, the new Jerusalem, coming down out of heaven from God, prepared as a bride beautifully dressed for her husband. And I heard a loud voice from the throne saying, "Look!

God's dwelling place is now among the people, and he will dwell with them. They will be his people, and God himself will be with them and be their God. 'He will wipe every tear from their eyes. There will be no more death' or mourning or crying or pain, for the old order of things has passed away."

He who was seated on the throne said, "I am making everything new!" Then he said, "Write this down, for these words are trustworthy and true."

He said to me: "It is done. I am the Alpha and the Omega, the Beginning and the End. To the thirsty I will give water without cost from the spring of the water of life. Those who are victorious will inherit all this, and I will be their God and they will be my children. But the cowardly, the unbelieving, the vile, the murderers, the sexually immoral, those who practice magic arts, the idolaters and all liars— they will be consigned to the fiery lake of burning sulfur. This is the second death."

One of the seven angels who had the seven bowls full of the seven last plagues came and said to me, "Come, I will show you the bride, the wife of the Lamb." And he carried me away in the Spirit to a mountain great and high, and showed me the Holy City, Jerusalem, coming down out of heaven from God. It shone with the glory of

God, and its brilliance was like that of a very precious jewel, like a jasper, clear as crystal. It had a great, high wall with twelve gates, and with twelve angels at the gates. On the gates were written the names of the twelve tribes of Israel. There were three gates on the east, three on the north, three on the south and three on the west. The wall of the city had twelve foundations, and on them were the names of the twelve apostles of the Lamb.

The angel who talked with me had a measuring rod of gold to measure the city, its gates and its walls. The city was laid out like a square, as long as it was wide. He measured the city with the rod and found it to be 12,000 stadia in length, and as wide and high as it is long. The angel measured the wall using human measurement, and it was 144 cubits thick. The wall was made of jasper, and the city of pure gold, as pure as glass. The foundations of the city walls were decorated with every kind of precious stone. The first foundation was jasper, the second sapphire, the third agate, the fourth emerald, the fifth onyx, the sixth ruby, the seventh chrysolite, the eighth beryl, the ninth topaz, the tenth turquoise, the eleventh jacinth, and the twelfth amethyst. The twelve gates were twelve pearls, each gate made of a single pearl. The great street of the city was of gold, as pure as transparent glass.

I did not see a temple in the city, because the Lord God Almighty and the Lamb are its temple. The city does not need the sun or the moon to shine on it, for the glory of God gives it light, and the Lamb is its lamp. The nations will walk by its light, and the kings of the earth will bring their splendor into it. On no day will its gates ever be shut, for there will be no night there. The glory and honor of the nations will be brought into it. Nothing impure will ever enter it, nor will anyone who does what is shameful or deceitful, but only those whose names are written in the Lamb's book of life.

What a beautiful description of things to come. God is actively restoring everything. That includes who we are as His children.

We can trust God with our heartache and rest on the fact that He is the restorer of all that the enemy stole, and we can look forward in hope for things to come. We move from a prodigal to a child of God. Our birthright all along. We go from a temporary place that we are just passing through to a beautiful eternal inheritance. A place that Jesus Himself is preparing for us. Once we begin to see the exchange of our lives full of heartache and sin for something so beautiful with Jesus, we begin to want to share about Jesus with others. We want to tell everyone about His unbelievable healing power and relationship. This, my friends, is called our testimony, and Scripture encourages us, as overcomers, to share it. Let's find out about the power of our testimony in the next chapter.

Reflection

Let's dive into something deep, the story of the prodigal son. When you read that story, what stirs in your heart? Can you feel the emotions, the joy of the son returning home? Now think about your eternal inheritance with God. Do you see Him as that Father, throwing a celebration when His children come home? Or perhaps you've pictured Him as distant, even angry at your past? It's an important question worth pondering.

Here's a challenge for you: ask God how you perceive Him. If you've been seeing Him in a way that doesn't quite match the loving Father in the story, it's time to set things straight. Ask Him to reveal His true nature to you, to show you that your real home is with Him. The way to see God clearly is to spend time reading His Word every day.

So, here's your call to action: take a moment, have that conversation with God. Let's reshape the way you see Him and rediscover the joy of coming home to your true Father. To embrace the inheritance He is preparing for you. Ready to make that connection?

CHAPTER 11

The Power of Testimony

"They triumphed over him by the blood of the Lamb
and by the word of their testimony; they did not
love their lives so much as to shrink from death."
~ Revelation 12:11

Testimony can sometimes be a scary word for believers. We wonder if we even have one. Would anyone care to listen if we did? I have seen people freeze in fear when they are asked to share their testimony. I know I have. It's such a vulnerable position, but it's something I encourage you to overcome.

Why is it so scary? It's your story, after all; it's not like being asked something we know nothing about. We are simply sharing what Jesus did in our lives while encouraging others to have faith in Jesus too.

So much of our testimonies is birthed out of the hard places we walked through, and maybe it's hard to relive it. Sometimes we are still in bondage to the pain that happened to us. Maybe it was a place we hoped to forget. Here's the thing, though: the more we tell our stories, the more we gain God's confidence and see His strength in them. We bring them from the dark corners of our hearts, where the devil wants to trap us, and into the light of Jesus, where they have power. This is where we become free.

You might be wondering what the word *testimony* even means. A testimony is a word, an oath, statement, or eyewitness to an event, proving something is true and it happened. It brings evidence to support something. We see this term used in the legal world a lot. The Bible also speaks about testimonies. What is the Bible referring to when it talks about a testimony?

While we read the eyewitness accounts about Jesus in the Scriptures, these compelling stories help us to know Jesus and what He did in others' lives. Similarly, our stories speak to who Jesus is and what He did in our lives. Our stories bring evidence to support who Jesus is too. Romans 10:17 says, "Consequently, faith comes from hearing the message, and the message is heard through the word about Christ." Our faith is built when we hear the Word of God and when we listen to other people's testimonies about what God did in their lives. Here we can ask ourselves the question, if Jesus did that for them, can He do it for me? My faith is even built when I share what God did in my own life; it never gets old! Our testimonies are the intricate threads in the fabric of our faith.

Immediately after Brennen passed away and Jesus entered my pain alongside me, I began to experience His peace, comfort, healing, and love, and that became part of my testimony. He transformed me in a supernatural way. I can't explain how He did it, but I became entirely changed when I allowed Him into my situation.

This is a benefit of the Holy Spirit living in us. He empowers us to be bold and share what happened. We offer what we have, and He supernaturally does a miracle with it. Think of the loaves and fishes' story in Matthew 14:17–19: "'We have here only five loaves of bread and two fish,' they answered. 'Bring them here to me,' he said. And he directed the people to sit down on the grass. Taking the five loaves and the two fish and looking up to heaven, he gave thanks and broke the loaves. Then he gave them to the disciples, and the disciples gave them to the people."

I remember one night when this scripture became alive in me. I attended a night of worship with a mission organization called Mountain Gateway. The founder, Britt Hancock, shared this verse, and this is what he wanted us to see: Jesus did the miracle with the loaves and fishes once they offered Jesus all they had. Jesus performed a miraculous feeding with five loaves and two fish, so that means our own stories of heartache can undergo a supernatural transformation when surrendered to Him as well. We give Him what little we have, and He supernaturally multiples it to help others.

They only found five loaves of bread and a couple of fish. How often do we feel like that? "This is all I have, Jesus. What can I come close to doing with it?" Well, we can't do much. It's when the disciples gave Jesus all they brought, and He blessed it and broke it and handed it back to them that the miracle happened.

The beauty of the loaves and fishes' story is not only in the miracle of what Jesus multiplied but also in the disciples' act of offering what little they held. It's a profound lesson for us during our own trials. While we bring our pain, our brokenness, and our suffering to Jesus, much like the disciples offered their loaves and fish, He performs a supernatural exchange.

We question if our story matters, but when we let Jesus transform our story, it is filled with power and purpose. Imagine what He can do with your painful story. I told Jesus that I couldn't do it on my own, so I offered what little I had left to Him. In my brokenness He blessed me and gave me back my story. This time it was touched by Jesus and became a dynamic testimony to feed others with. Our story multiplies in exponential ways.

It feeds others with hope, healing, and faith in Jesus. It transforms us and others. Just as the disciples witnessed a miracle unfold with their simple offerings, we, too, can witness the miraculous transformation of our pain into a testimony that brings restoration and redemption. The loaves and fishes' story, therefore, becomes a mighty reminder that our painful offerings, when surrendered to Jesus, can be the catalyst for a divine exchange that multiplies beyond our wildest imaginations.

We bring our ashes, and He makes them into something beautiful because His healing presence is always with us. Isaiah 61:3 says God will "bestow on them a crown of beauty instead of ashes, the oil of joy instead of mourning, and a garment of praise instead of a spirit of despair."

To bestow something on someone means to give something as an honor or gift. Do you see what He does when we allow Him into our broken places? He exchanges them for beauty, joy, and praise! Our spirits are clothed in these things. Only God can do this! Like I shared regarding the story of Job, we no longer just have head knowledge of Jesus from stories we've heard; we have firsthand experience with who Jesus is for ourselves.

Just as I shared my story about how Jesus carried me through loss, it also became my testimony about who Jesus is, including His faithfulness, His peace, His comfort, and His healing power. Jesus was no longer just someone I read about in the Bible; He became someone I experienced personally. I share my testimony to give others hope too. Psalm 18:2 describes what Jesus became for me: "The Lord is my rock, my fortress and my deliverer; my God is my rock, in whom I take refuge, my shield and the horn of my salvation, my stronghold."

Hearing others' testimonies spurs us on to believe that if God can do it for them, He can do it for me! The Bible is full of testimonies that confirm what I experienced by knowing Jesus, and it's even more amazing to see that my testimony is added to all those testimonies who have encountered the living God. The apostles shared in Acts 4:33, "With great power the apostles continued to testify to the resurrection of the Lord Jesus. And God's grace was so powerfully at work in them all."

God also speaks to us through other people's testimonies. Each person is carrying a piece of a puzzle to the much bigger story of God. Testimonies reveal God's character, love, faithfulness, healing, miracles, and revelations. Testimonies record what God does from one generation to another. Testimonies are real-life stories of our encounters with Jesus and of His power working in us and through us. While we share our stories, our faith grows, our understanding of God grows, and we gain more revelation about His heart.

The death and resurrection of Jesus is where our testimony starts as a believer. Over our lifetime, however, we have countless testimonies in our walk with Jesus. I believe it's important to grasp what God was doing in our lives in these stories so we can share them at the right moments. You never know when you will need to share one of your stories to help someone else. Like I mentioned above, your first testimony is usually how you met Jesus—your salvation experience. Who you were before knowing Him and how you changed after knowing Him. This describes your sanctification process. This process is how you become more like Christ. This is very persuasive because people don't tend to argue about your experiences. The Bible says in 2 Corinthians 3:18 "And we all, who with unveiled faces contemplate the Lord's glory, are being transformed into his image with ever-increasing glory, which comes from the Lord, who is the Spirit." These testimonies range from the smallest of details to big, all-powerful miracles.

I remember when I prayed about writing this book. I wanted to make sure God was asking me to do it and not just something I wanted to do. I carried a nudging for a long time that one day I would write this book. Then one year I felt the prompting of the Holy Spirit that it was time. I began to ask God to give me a sign that He for sure wanted me to do this. Something no one would have knowledge of is that we gave Brennen the nickname Bumblebee. I can't be the only one who comes up with fun little nicknames for my children and pets!

The week I asked God for a sign, I also attended an all-night prayer meeting at my church. That night I met a girl for the first time. Obviously, she didn't know about my story. While she prayed with me, she said God showed her a bee when she looked at me. She asked, "I realize this is weird, but does this mean anything to you?" I laughed and shared the story with her. This built her faith about hearing from God clearly and my faith that He is in the details of my life. And He had given me the sign I asked for.

After that night I started seeing bumblebees everywhere: on a coffee mug, a pillow in the store, and on a bag at another store. I was like, "Okay, God, I get it. I have the green light to write the book!" Of course, this entire book is a compelling testimony of how God takes our pain, suffering, afflictions, and trials and heals us, sets us free, and empowers us to go on.

How we live our lives demonstrates an influential testimony as well. When others see our dedication to God (even in our suffering), they want to learn more about Him. What we truly believe about Jesus will determine the course of our lives. How we spend our time, our resources, our words, and approach to everything should point others to Jesus. We should be reflecting Jesus's character in everything we do. Our lifestyles are persuasive testimonies because people will want to fathom how you are able to live the way you do. They will be curious about the change that took place in your life.

It's the power of the Holy Spirit in us that allows us to live differently than those around us. When we choose love over hate, forgiveness over unforgiveness, dying to our flesh instead of giving in, patience instead of annoyance etc., these are the testimonies with Jesus that make the world take notice.

One of the most impressive fruits we get to experience is once we have walked through our pain in Jesus, we get to sit down with another person who is where we once stood. I can't tell you how many times I have had the opportunity to minister to someone in their pain while sharing my story. This is why our testimony is so impactful. You are drowning in your pain and mess, and along comes someone who speaks life into you and your situation. Someone who has been there and knows the power of Jesus.

Sharing with another person in pain allows them to see how Jesus worked in your story— it gives them a front row seat. This could be a lightbulb moment for them when they begin to see the hope of Jesus. They begin to realize that if God did that for you, then maybe He can do that for them. Something comes alive in them. They start to reach for Jesus's outstretched hand.

I remember years ago when I encountered the opportunity to share my story with another hurting mom. I took a job as a long-term substitute teacher at my daughter's school. I would work in whatever classroom they needed me or in the office. Not something I wanted to do, but the job came about because I had a teaching degree. After I took the job, I realized there would be more to the story.

That year a second-grade teacher lost her baby. The baby had been stillborn. When she came back to work, I knew the Holy Spirit wanted me to share my story. Obediently, I did. I remember us crying and hugging together. She felt the hope of Jesus when we talked. What I didn't comprehend in that moment was this experience also became a healing point in my journey. It was when my story became His story. What He did in it. The Holy Spirit's presence in me gave me the confidence and strength to share my story with another hurting person who was walking a similar road I had walked—and it felt empowering.

When I perceived the Holy Spirit telling me to write this book, I didn't have context at that point of even when or how. It was just an idea. I wondered, "What if it comes off like I'm trying to promote myself." Struggling with these thoughts, I heard undoubtedly from

God that this book is His story, not my story. Yes, I lived it, but what He did with it was all about Him! I'm more than happy to give Him the glory!

In Revelation 12:11 we read, "They triumphed over him by the blood of the Lamb and by the word of their testimony; they did not love their lives so much as to shrink from death." Who do we triumph over? We triumph over Satan when we receive the blood of Jesus Christ and what He did on the cross, but also by the word of our testimony.

Every time we read the testimony of the Bible, listen to others' testimonies, and share ours, we build our faith, learn wisdom and revelation, and grow deeper roots in Jesus. We link our testimonies together and become overcomers in our hard situations and over the enemy, who wants nothing more than to put a wedge between us and Jesus.

We are called to shine the light of Jesus and illuminate His mighty works in each of our sufferings. Telling how Jesus steps in and changes the course of our circumstances, the course of our lives, and the course of our destinies shows the world how compassionate, loving, and redemptive He is. Our testimonies show how the enemy's power has been stripped away.

Colossians 2:12–16 proves this, "having been buried with him in baptism, in which you were also raised with him through your faith in the working of God, who raised him from the dead. When you were dead in your sins and in the uncircumcision of your flesh, God made you alive with Christ. He forgave us all our sins, having canceled the charge of our legal indebtedness, which stood against us and condemned us; he has taken it away, nailing it to the cross. And having disarmed the powers and authorities, he made a public spectacle of them, triumphing over them by the cross."

Jesus disarmed the enemy and made a public spectacle of the devil. This should spur us on even more to triumph and take hold of all that Jesus has for us. He gave us the tools to overcome: the blood of the Lamb and word of our testimony!

Does the thought of sharing your testimony scare you? Let me share what Shelby Abbott from the Gospel Coalition says about our testimonies: "In over two decades working as a full-time minister, I've learned that personal testimonies are one of the most influential tools the Holy Spirit uses to stir spiritual interest and point people toward Christ. There's no more poignant and dynamic way to communicate the gospel than by sharing your story—not because we're so amazing, but because Jesus is so glorious."[5] I agree with her statement. I have seen the same thing over the years as I have shared and as I have listened to other testimonies.

Below are a few tips on how to share your testimony. Before long you'll feel empowered by the Holy Spirit and be able share your story in the spur of a moment without much thought. The best way almost always comes through building relationships with others. This is a natural way to share about Jesus. The Bible states, "Always be prepared to give an answer to everyone who asks you to give the reason for the hope that you have" (1 Peter 3:15). We are called to share our testimony about Jesus.

> *Keep it short and simple. Three to five minutes gives the listener enough time to respond. It isn't important that every detail be in the story. You are simply having a conversation with someone; this is not the time for a three-point sermon.

---

[5] Shelby Abbott, "6 Principles for Sharing Your Testimony," The Gospel Coalition, June 1, 2021, https://www.thegospelcoalition.org/article/sharing-your-testimony/.

*Talk about who you were before you met Jesus and who you are now. This is about what He changed in you, and this is the point.

*Stick to the central point. Again, who you were before you met Jesus and how He changed your life.

*Always share the gospel. Who Jesus is. Our testimonies should always point to Him.

*Practice sharing with someone you are comfortable with. This will help let your guard down, and you'll learn what needs to be tweaked when you do this.

Allowing Jesus to heal our painful stories is how they become influential testimonies. This is why it matters. Let's fix our eyes on what He did for us and on the power that He carries to heal us—not on the fear or uncertainty we may have of sharing. Besides, He is the author and finisher of our stories. Do you feel stuck in heartache and despair? Then apprehend this—Jesus isn't finished with your story! Hebrews 12:2 says, "fixing our eyes on Jesus, the pioneer and perfecter of faith. For the joy set before him he endured the cross, scorning its shame, and sat down at the right hand of the throne of God."

Ask Jesus to provide the strength needed to bring you through the hurt and to become an eyewitness for His healing. Once you get to a place where you share your testimony, you will begin to walk in a greater freedom, greater trust, and greater authority in Jesus.

Our stories are a transformative force in the life of each of us as believers. When we understand the significance of sharing our stories, we discover that testimonies are not just personal stories; they are capable tools that showcase the faithfulness, love, power, restoration, healing, and redemptive power of Jesus Christ.

Testimonies, as shown in Revelation 12:11, are our triumph over the enemy. The blood of the Lamb, symbolizing the sacrifice of Jesus on the cross, is the foundation of our victory. The word of our testimony is the faith amplifying this truth. When we share our stories, we become overcomers, breaking the attacks of the enemy and testifying to the all-powerful work of Jesus.

Our testimonies not only strengthen our faith but also serve as hope for others. By exchanging our ashes for beauty, we become those who carry God's healing presence. Letting go of our brokenness for God's supernatural love allows us to become like the loaves and fishes' story, where we offer our brokenness to Jesus and He turns it into a powerful testimony to feed others.

The impact of testimonies goes beyond personal encounters; they reveal God's character, love, faithfulness, and miracles. Sharing our stories means we contribute to the tapestry of God's work from one generation to another. Our faith is built not only by hearing the Word of God but also by hearing the testimonies of what God does in the lives of all believers.

The call to share our testimonies is not just a recommendation but a command to shine the light of Jesus. Our lifestyles become testimonies, pointing others to Christ through our actions, choices, and worship to Him. We are encouraged to reflect Jesus's character in everything we do, becoming living testimonies that draw others to us because they, too, want to experience the source of our transformation.

Finally, the ultimate mandate is to fix our eyes on Jesus, the author and finisher of our faith. Regardless of the pain and despair we may be experiencing, Jesus is not finished with our stories. By allowing Him to provide the strength needed to walk through our hurts, we become eyewitnesses of His power. When we share our testimonies, we not only experience greater freedom, trust, and authority in Jesus but also break the enemy's strongholds in our lives and help others do the same.

So, let us be bold in sharing our testimonies, knowing that they carry the potential to spur on, encourage, and bring hope to those who need to encounter the transformative power of Jesus. I have a question for you: do you think it matters how you suffer? You probably discerned by now it does. We are after the fruit of the Spirit which springs forth in us and the inheritance that only Jesus can provide as we trade our pain for Him. It does matter how we go through hard times. I'm not talking about having a bad day in your hurt; I'm talking about where we end up is everything. Our perspective changes how we walk through this journey. Let's take a look at how Jesus walked through suffering so that we can grasp how to suffer well. Remember, in this world people suffer to suffer because of the fallen nature we live in. Not us, though! We have Jesus, and our suffering produces something better in us that can only come from Him.

Reflection

Think of the moment you gave your life to Jesus and begin to journal your testimony. How did it happen? What did you experience? When did it happen? Formulate your story so you are comfortable sharing it with someone who might need to hear it. You should do this each time Jesus does something in your life. Keep a book of remembrance. Remember, our walk with Jesus will have many testimonies over time. "Be prepared in season and out of season," is what the Bible says in 2 Timothy 4:2. Using the tips above that were shared, have your testimony ready so that in a moment's notice you feel confident to share with someone else what Jesus did in your life and to encourage them in what they are going through.

CHAPTER 12

Suffering Well

*"God had one son on earth without sin,
but never one without suffering."*
~ Saint Augustine

I was standing in my bathroom one morning getting ready for church when I heard the Holy Spirit saying, "Tell her to 'suffer well.' Tell her the last major blow to the enemy is to suffer well in me. Tell her to set her mind on things above and keep her faith in Jesus, to praise Jesus despite what she is going through." I had been praying for my mom when I discerned these words to tell her.

My mom had been diagnosed with breast cancer over four years before that prayer. She had been healed, and we had four beautiful years with her. Then in June of 2023 we got the news that her scans showed the cancer was back. The doctors found spots on her lungs and liver. When I took hold of those words—*suffer well*—that morning in the bathroom, it was already nearing the end of August.

That same day I shared them with my mom when I went to visit her in the hospital. Her lungs had kept filling up with fluid from the cancer, and she would have to go into the hospital to have them drained. She was so tired and weak. She said the words I shared resonated with her. The Holy Spirit was encouraging her how to fight this battle. The first time she was diagnosed, I had felt like it was a fight against the enemy who had come to steal, kill, and destroy, according to John 10:10, but God healed her. This time around things were different.

I remember the first time she got diagnosed the Holy Spirit told me to "flood it with the light." Meaning, pray God's words over the situation and bind up this spirit of infirmity. This time around the situation with my mom felt different in my spirit. It felt like I was being prepared to let go. She sensed that this was going to be her time to go home to be with Jesus.

When I heard "suffer well," she had been on the battlefield of surrendering it all to Jesus—it was hard to see her go through that. Knowing you're coming to the end of your life and working it out in Jesus is no easy task. It's truly a battle to lay it all at His feet in complete trust; it's our ultimate surrender.

Our last great battle here on earth is facing death. Our mind receives blows from the enemy filled fear and what-ifs. But Jesus gave us His word that we have the mind of Christ. First Corinthians 2:16 says, "Who has known the mind of the Lord so as to instruct him? But we have the mind of Christ." Jesus's life is our life, because we are united with Jesus, which means we have His mind and have victory over death. The Bible is the Word of God, and Jesus is the Word made flesh. The battlefield in our mind is where we overcome the enemy or give in to his tactics to keep our faith and confidence away from God. We can only survive this assault when we know His Word, stay in prayer, and praise Him. We must set our affections on Jesus during the battle.

Here's the thing: when we are faced with death, it's not that we don't want to be with Jesus; the hard part is the fear and sadness of what we are leaving behind. My mom cried countless tears over her grandchildren and her soon-to-be-born great-grandbaby due in October 2023. She said, "I only want to make it to meet my great-grand girl," as she lovingly called her. Of course, she didn't want to leave her daughters behind either. The only things that matter in the end are your family and friends and what we believe about Jesus.

First Thessalonians 4:13 says, "Brothers and sisters, we do not want you to be uniformed about those who sleep in death, so that you do not grieve like the rest of mankind, who have no hope." This scripture assures us that as believers we will reunite with our loved ones again. Jesus took away the sting of death when He paid for our sins on the cross. We still physically die; it's a consequence of sin. But one day that will be done away with, for Jesus has the keys of death. Revelation 1:18 tells us: "I am the Living One; I was dead, and now look, I am alive for ever and ever! And I hold the keys to death and Hades." We don't have to fear death because of what Jesus did for us on the cross. First Corinthians 15:54–55 says, "Death has been swallowed up in victory. Where, O death, is your victory? Where, O death, is your sting?"

As Jesus suffered, He took it all away. The story didn't end when Jesus died—He rose on the third day! For believers, we will share the same resurrection story as Jesus did. Romans 6:23 tells us, "For the wages of sin is death, but the gift of God is eternal life in Christ Jesus our Lord." Look at what 1 Corinthians 15:42–49 says about resurrection:

> So will it be with the resurrection of the dead. The body that is sown is perishable, it is raised imperishable; it is sown in dishonor, it is raised in glory; it is sown in weakness, it is raised in power; it is sown a natural body, it is raised a spiritual body. If there is a natural body, there is also a spiritual body. So it is written: "The first man Adam became a living being"; the last Adam, a life-giving spirit. The spiritual did not

come first, but the natural, and after that the spiritual. The first man was of the dust of the earth; the second man is of heaven. As was the earthly man, so are those who are of the earth; and as is the heavenly man, so also are those who are of heaven. And just as we have borne the image of the earthly man, so shall we bear the image of the heavenly man.

In this book, we have walked on a journey that has shown us the fruit of trading our pain and heartache for a greater purpose in Jesus—what He gives us instead. Let's keep going so we can finish well and be kingdom builders for Him.

What does suffering well mean anyway? Jesus gave us the perfect model. It wasn't that He wanted to suffer; it's that He understood it was the only way. He was willing to suffer for the cause of bringing us back into right relationship with God. He knew it was the only sacrifice that would pay for the sins of the world and bring us back in right standing with God. Jesus had asked His Father in Matthew 26:39, "My Father, if it is possible, may this cup be taken from me. Yet not as I will, but as you will." Jesus had to go through suffering to be resurrected.

Jesus had to get up on the cross. If we are going to identify in His resurrection, then we are also going to have to identify with His suffering. First Peter 4:13 says, "But rejoice inasmuch as you participate in the sufferings of Christ, so that you may be overjoyed when his glory is revealed." Second Corinthians 1:5 tells us, "For just as we share abundantly in the sufferings of Christ, so also our comfort abounds through Christ."

If Jesus is our model on how to suffer well, what can we learn from Him? The first thing that stands out to me is that He was willing to be obedient to the Father's plan. Jesus prayed for the will of the Father to be done, not His own. He trusted the Father's will. Jesus wanted everything He did to glorify God the Father. He knew that what we go through here on earth shapes us to be like Him. We are not happy about suffering, and neither was Jesus. But we can be happy about what we gain from it when we are surrendered to Jesus.

Jesus's suffering on the cross resulted in redemption for us. When we suffer well, we allow God to be glorified. This changes our perspective and helps others to grasp what God has done in us. First Peter 2:20–24 tells us,

> But how is it to your credit if you receive a beating for doing wrong and endure it? But if you suffer for doing good and you endure it, this is commendable before God. To this you were called, because Christ suffered for you, leaving you an example, that you should follow in his steps. "He committed no sin, and no deceit was found in his mouth." When they hurled their insults at him, he did not retaliate; when he suffered, he made no threats. Instead, he entrusted himself to him who judges justly. He himself bore our sins in his body on the cross, so that we might die to sins and live for righteousness; "by his wounds you have been healed."

When we accept that God is for us, that He loves us and wants the best for us, we can begin to understand the consequences of living in a fallen world where bad things happen, but from that God can bring beauty from our ashes. This acceptance is about surrendering our lives to trusting in our Father God. That's what Jesus did in the above scripture. He entrusted Himself to God *through* the suffering.

The next thing we notice is Jesus kept His eyes on the bigger picture. He comprehended that what He was going through was temporary, not eternal. However, it did have eternal implications. In Randy Acorn's book *Heaven*, he says, "Anticipating heaven doesn't eliminate pain, but it lessons it and puts it in perspective. Meditating on heaven is a great pain reliever. It reminds us that suffering and death are temporary conditions. Our existence will not end in suffering and death—they are but a gateway to our eternal life of unending joy."[6]

Our perception is important. We have been given the mind of Christ to see the bigger picture and to seek God's will above our own. We have His Word to read and His Spirit in us to remind us of all truth. We know how the story of mankind will end: Jesus restores it all eventually! While we are here on the earth, the restoration process has already started. But just like Jesus, we have to endure the suffering; but also just like Jesus, we have the tools to trust and desire the will of God.

Also, when we choose to suffer well like Jesus, it causes others to wonder about Jesus. We become His witnesses. There is something about suffering in Christ that causes people to take notice. Through His love, He draws our hearts to Him. When we suffer well in the hard things, we become grateful instead of bitter, and this gives others a reason to go to God too. They want to know how we can keep peace and joy and an eternal perspective in the suffering. This gives us an open door to share with others who Jesus is. Remember, it becomes your testimony!

So, what are we teaching people in our suffering? When we suffer well it advances the gospel, proving the power of the cross to others and drawing them to the feet of Jesus. Paul gave us an amazing example of this in Philippians 1:12–14: "Now I want you

---

6   Randy Acorn, *Heaven: A Comprehensive Guide to Everything the Bible Says About Our Eternal Home* (Carol Stream, IL: Tyndale Momentum, 2004), 460.

to know, brothers and sisters, that what has happened to me has actually served to advance the gospel. As a result, it has become clear throughout the whole palace guard and to everyone else that I am in chains for Christ. And because of my chains, most of the brothers and sisters have become confident in the Lord and dare all the more to proclaim the gospel without fear."

Paul wasn't hyper focused on being in prison; he saw the bigger picture and knew that this needed to happen to advance the gospel. He remembered that all things work together for the good of those who love Him (Romans 8:28).

Lastly, when we suffer well in Christ and are comforted by Him, this helps us keep our focus on others and not so much on the situation. Jesus's focus was always on others. God wants us to do the same. Not too long ago I was chatting on the phone with my son, Nate, who was eighteen at the time and living out of the country on the mission field with an organization called YWAM. It was 5:00 a.m. my time and about 10:00 p.m. his time. I was telling him how bad things were looking in our state at that moment. The border tension was high, and no one was seeing eye to eye. We also talked about wars breaking out in the Middle East. Things seemed grim. He was not seeing the news since he was in a remote location. As we talked, he stopped me as I was telling him all the bad things and said we needed to pray. Then he said: "Mom, who cares if there is war all over the world. Our mission doesn't change!"

Now, of course he didn't mean who cares that there is war; he meant that there has been conflict since the beginning of time, and all throughout history there have been times of stability and safety and periods of instability and chaos. His point was that no matter what is going on, our mission with Jesus does not change! Being on mission with Jesus and joining in on His plans are exactly what Jesus is calling us to. We are to keep our focus on Jesus so that He can help us keep our focus on serving others and sharing the gospel. Matthew 20:28

says, "The Son of Man did not come to be served, but to serve, and to give His life as a ransom for many."

When we walk well in Jesus through the suffering, we get to comfort others and share about Jesus. Second Corinthians 1:3–4 says, "Praise be to the God and Father of our Lord Jesus Christ, the Father of compassion and the God of all comfort, who comforts us in all our troubles, so that we can comfort those in any trouble with the comfort we ourselves receive from God."

I know from my own suffering that I met God in the deepest ways. He showed me who He is time and again. One of the greatest blessings that comes from our suffering is to know Him better. There is a song titled "O Come to the Altar" by the band Elevation that reminds us to handle what we are going through *with Jesus* as we wait for Him to return. He will right every wrong! Jesus is our treasure here on earth as we wait for our eternal rewards. What do we do while we wait? Share His testimony and yours with the world!

If you remember at the beginning of this chapter, I told my mom that suffering well was the last blow to the enemy. The battle over the enemy is won in our mind-set. Our perception and thoughts become everything. What are you focusing on? Who are your thoughts on? The battle is always in our minds no matter what we go through or endure. No matter what we face.

I remember when my mom was in pain toward the end of her life and she would say to me, "I remind myself that what Jesus went through was so much more than me." Over time she battled the enemy and surrendered to trusting Jesus. Her words still resonate in my thoughts. I want to suffer well this side of eternity so that I can have victory over the enemy and receive the blessings of restoration and purpose in Jesus, like my mom.

I also want to look Jesus in the eye one day and receive the crown of life. Revelation 2:10 reminds us, "Do not be afraid of what you are about to suffer. I tell you, the devil will put some of you in prison to test you, and you will suffer persecution for ten days. Be faithful, even to the point of death, and I will give you life as your victor's crown." This crown of life will be for all who have endured sufferings and persecutions, some even to the point of death. The key is always to move closer to Jesus through every trial and tribulation we encounter.

Our mind-set while suffering is what Jesus came to transform because that is where true freedom is found. Romans 12:2, "Do not conform to the pattern of this world, but be transformed by the renewing of your mind. Then you will be able to test and approve what God's will is-his good, pleasing and perfect will." This is where our perception is changed for the good. We trade our faulty mind-sets and beliefs for the truth of God's Word. We pull down the lies that the enemy has sown in us and silence his voice once and for all. We cannot live in freedom and healing if we are not immersed in the Word of God. This allows the Word of God to define our thoughts and experiences, not our experiences to define God. As our minds become like the mind of Christ, we start to live from this place; God's will becomes our desire.

In an article by Marshall Segal entitled "How to Suffer Well: Three Ways to Prepare Now," Don Carson has some wise words regarding suffering: "One of the major causes of devastating grief and confusion among Christians is that our expectations are false.... We do not give the subject of evil and suffering the thought it deserves until we ourselves are confronted with tragedy." Segal continues, "No one falls into the stunning ability to be 'sorrowful' and yet, at the same time, 'always rejoicing' (2 Corinthians 6:10) without first patiently, even tenaciously, seeking God. If we want to suffer well, we need to learn where to stand, and where to look, when our storms come—and we do well to learn *before* they come."[7]

---

[7] Marshall Segal, "How to Suffer Well:Three Ways to Prepare Now," desiringGod.org, February 21, 2020, https://www.desiringgod.org/articles/how-to-suffer-well.

This has a lot to do with our expectations. We often stay in bondage because of the expectations we place upon our lives. We need to learn to live in the reality of our situations and not our expectations. It's helpful to have some scriptures to stand on as our foundation so when storms come, we aren't completely taken out.

We have a choice to make in how we will perceive what we go through. Will we allow our circumstances to define us? Or will we allow Jesus to define us? Our identity, authority, and purpose are at stake if we don't process our hurts with Jesus. We will find ourselves stuck in the enemy's territory roaming around as if in a prison.

There is no freedom if we stay here. Jesus is calling each of us to a place of freedom. A place of healing and wholeness. A place where His manifest presence of peace is always with us. A place where He brings beauty from ashes and wisdom that can only come from a sovereign God. Here, we receive an anointing that cannot be touched by the enemy because we have been through the fire and come out with the aroma and light of Jesus—to carry His message into the world.

Taking Jesus's hand invites us into so much more than this world can throw at us or even offer. Our souls need to be anchored to Jesus, not tossed back and forth by the waves of life. Matthew 8:23–27 tells us, "Then he got into the boat and his disciples followed him. Suddenly a furious storm came up on the lake, so that waves swept over the boat. But Jesus was sleeping. The disciples went and woke him, saying, 'Lord, save us! We're going to drown!' He replied, 'You of little faith, why are you so afraid?' Then he got up and rebuked the winds and the waves, and it was completely calm. The men were amazed and asked, 'What kind of man is this? Even the winds and the waves obey him.'"

Jesus didn't sleep because He didn't care. He slept because He wasn't worried. He trusted the storm wouldn't hurt Him. In fact, He had the power to calm the storm. He was in perfect control then and is in control now. We are called to rest in Jesus and know that His power can calm any storm. This is where hope begins.

Charles Spurgeon is a well-known minister who lived during the 1800s in London. He is noted for being well acquainted with suffering. He suffered with illnesses and depression while pastoring the largest mega church in Protestant Christendom. According to Spurgeon.Org, "Spurgeon's ministry sparked a wildfire throughout the world because it was forged, to be sure, in the fire. 'I think it would have been less painful to have been burned alive at the stake than to have passed through those horrors and depressions of spirit' .... Yet even in the heat of public criticism, character assassination, physical setbacks, and emotional challenges, Spurgeon experienced the warm kindness of God. Spurgeon never suffered from having never suffered. He saw hardships as God's hammer, shaping sinners into holiness and channeled his suffering into his sermons. He said, 'You must go through the fire ... if you would have sympathy with others who tread the glowing coals.'"[8]

Spurgeon was called to serve others as a minister. He suffered and allowed that to draw him closer to Jesus, not away from Him. He understood what it was to suffer well and to serve others from this place. He kept his eyes on the bigger picture of salvation and the gospel message. He knew he was only on the earth temporarily.

In Joshua Giles's book *Mantled for Greatness*, he writes,

> God is not fair, but He is just, which means He will balance out the scales for you. He is the God who will put a coat on one and not the other. Ask Joseph's father. God said, 'Jacob I have loved, but Esau I have hated' (Malachi

---

[8] "10 Spurgeon Quotes for Wounded Christians," September 6, 2016, Spurgeon. org, https://www.spurgeon.org/resource-library/blog-entries/10-spurgeon-quotes-for-wounded-christians/.

1:2–3; Romans 9:13). What he was saying, in essence, was that I put My hand on Jacob, but I rejected Esau because of purpose. Jacob put that coat on Joseph, but the other sons seemed to feel as though they were rejected. Yet it was about purpose. It wasn't personal. You have to understand that what you must go through for the anointing isn't personal. It may feel as though it is. If you take your life experience personally, you will be walking around angry at everybody, including God. This is why God must take you through a process of refinement and maturity. When we understand God's love for us and that His plan for our lives is good, the difficulties become easier to overcome. We see God's hand in each of those moments and understand His purpose for leading us through them because they were part of a bigger picture. We come out understanding how true it is that God turns those trying times around for our good. We come out delivered from pride into a place of total surrender. I'm telling you that if you can take it, you will pay the price for the anointing. And by the time you get through all of that, you will be ready for where God is taking you.[9]

I'm sure we have all been sensing something on the landscape. A spiritual shift, so to speak, in the world. Everything has changed since COVID for that was a defining moment across the earth. Everyone

---

[9] Joshua Giles, *Mantled for Greatness: Your Prophetic Guide to Releasing a God-Sized Dream* (Ada, MI: Chosen Books, 2023), 202.

146

has been affected one way or another. Some for the better, but some are still really struggling.

I want to call you to a higher place. I want you to begin to look at your story with a fresh set of eyes and ask Jesus to see it through His lens, with a purpose for the days ahead. When we go through hard things in Jesus, we get anointed for more, to take back territory from the enemy and put it back in right standing with Jesus. The spiritual landscape is changing. Are you ready?

Have you begun to walk out your pain with Jesus so you can be equipped for things to come? There is a harvest of souls for Jesus just waiting to know Him, to walk out their own pain with purpose. Who's going to tell them about taking Jesus's hand—if not us?

If we stay stuck in the loss and pain, then it's all for nothing—the enemy wins. But I don't want that to be your last chapter. I want you to overcome and lay it all down before Jesus so you can help others find their freedom in him. There is so much suffering and pain in the world. So much loss, deception, and hurt. But we know this doesn't have to be their story. We have a part to play, a piece of the puzzle for them. Let your loss be the treasure someone else gets to pick up. Let your story be the loaves and fishes that Jesus does a miracle with to feed others.

So, ultimately our eyes need to be on what we are doing for the kingdom of God. When we walk through our circumstances with Jesus, we are equipped to go out and share our testimony with others. We then become defined by Christ and not our circumstances. We carry the fruit that Jesus grew in us. We have endured and persevered and are ready to receive our inheritance.

Remember the following scripture from earlier: Luke 22:31–32. Read it as another key to overcoming our hardships and fiery ordeals. It says, "Simon, Simon, Satan has asked to sift all of you as wheat. But I have prayed for you, Simon, that your faith may not fail. And when you have turned back, strengthen your brothers."

147

What an amazing confidence that Jesus had in Simon. He said *when* you turn back, not *if* you turn back. As the world gets darker, we can be the ones on the front lines leading others to Jesus in their difficulties. We are the light in the darkest night carrying the answer of Jesus. We will be the ones shading others with our shade tree grown in faith. Others will be drawn to the essence of Jesus on us. We are the ones who have been set on fire for His glory—released to help the prodigals come home and see the heart of the Father.

Our testimony will spur them on to suffer well and in return have their own testimony in Jesus. Our prayers will sow the seed they need to take Jesus by the hand with confidence and strength. Jesus will become the true healer and redeemer of their stories. Our anointing comes out of our pain and suffering; this is our ministry. This is our testimony! We have the authority of Jesus living in us to be His hands and feet. To show others His compassion. So, how is God calling you to help others with your story?

Reflection

Think about the major storm that you are walking through? Take some time to reflect on the scriptures in this chapter. Next, ask God to show you how being an overcomer in this storm is equipping you to move forward to stand in the things to come. What could He be wanting to do with what you have walked through? How is this preparing you for things to come? This is where we can begin to dream of how we can be used to build God's kingdom and help others!

FINAL THOUGHTS

"Our Lord has written the promise of resurrection,
not in books alone, but in every leaf in springtime."
~ Martin Luther

As we come to the end of our journey together, I hope that my unthinkable story of brokenness and my walk hand in hand with Jesus through healing and restoration has given you a new perspective on the hard things you have walked through in your life. My heart is that wherever you are in your story that you surrender the pain to Jesus and take hold of His capable hand. He will lead you to true healing and bring purpose to your painful stories. But you must grab hold of His hand and accept His invitation to walk you through to the other side. He doesn't leave us in the dark places of pain, depression, fear, and anxiety. He leads us to resurrection life where we find freedom. But we have to trust Him through the process.

When God enters our painful experiences, hopelessness turns to hope, darkness turns to light, suffering brings forth purpose and fruit. Our pain is never wasted when we give it to Jesus. Jesus has so much compassion for each of us because He, too, suffered. Tucked away in John 11:35 there is a scripture that simply reads, "Jesus wept." It's so short but so profound. Jesus being fully man and God meant He felt our pain. He knows what it feels like to walk through hard times. To lose someone close.

That scripture of Jesus weeping is found in the story of Lazarus, a friend who died. Jesus was moved by grief and compassion. He was moved to bring him back to life. This is our story too. Jesus moves in compassion for us and all that we go through here on earth. He knows the devastation that sin brings. We all have the hope of the resurrection one day too. The Bible says in John 11: 25–26 Jesus said to her, "I am the resurrection and the life. The one who believes in me will live, even though they die; and whoever lives by believing in me will never die. Do you believe this?"

That's the question right there that changes the course of our lives and every painful story we have walked through. Do you believe this? Do you believe that Jesus can not only resurrect the dead but can also resurrect your painful stories and breathe new life into you? Do you believe this? How you answer and respond to Jesus will change the course of your story. Responding to Jesus will open the door to all that He has for you this side of eternity and on into eternity. As the pages of this book close, I pray that you will allow that question to sink into the core of your relationship with Jesus. And that your answer will take root in your story. I pray that with everything in you, you'll be able to say without a shadow of a doubt that "Yes Jesus, I believe you can do the impossible and you will bring life from my dead places. I believe in you Jesus here is my hand."

ABOUT THE AUTHOR

Heather Bradley is the founder of Truth: Freedom Ministry @truthfreedomministry, a social media ministry for women, to be equipped and encouraged in the things of God. She is passionate about helping people walk through the hard things of life. A Texas girl at heart but loves the adventure of going to new places. She has been married to the love of her life, Kelly, for over 29 years and they have 4 children. They homeschooled their kiddos and have lived all over the USA but are happy to be home in Austin during this season. You will typically find her serving at her local church, that they help plant, in pastoral care and women's ministry. She received her bachelor's degree in education. Later she attended Bible School and has been ordained in pastoral ministry. Heather love's gardening, reading books, trying new recipes, and her German Shepherd, Hank. Her favorite place to be is sitting down for coffee with others while listening to them share their life stories. The latest news is she is a first-time grandmother! So, her new name is Gigi! Heather co-host's a podcast, called Leaving the Shallows @leavingtheshallows, with her good friend—where they help listeners leave the shallow end of religion and go into the deeper things of Jesus. Her prayer is that others would know the love of Jesus in their hardest moments here on earth and experience His healing and purpose and know that He is always with them.

ACKNOWLEDGEMENTS

I never saw myself as a writer and would not have pursued writing this book if Jesus hadn't compelled me too. I knew I had a message to share though. I give Jesus all the glory and acknowledgments. As He reminded me this is His story to tell. I pray it gives Him all the glory and that it spurs every reader into the healing hands of Jesus and the purposes He has for each of you. My heart as you read this book is that you see Jesus.

Brennen, my baby, the one who brought me back to Jesus and gave me this message to share. I can't thank you enough for the sacrifice of your life and what it brought to my life. I can't wait to see you in heaven. You are always in my heart.

Kelly, my husband, who has given everything in this world to give me everything in my world. Thank you for always supporting me and spoiling me—there is no one like you! Love you always and forever.

Nadia, Nicolas, and Nathan, my children, who each taught me how to draw closer to God. You are my treasures on earth. My heart and my world. I love you each beyond measure. I wouldn't be who I am without each of you. Thanks for spurring me on and teaching me how to dig deep roots in Christ. I pray you each go further in the Kingdom of God than I could ever imagine.

Kinsley, my first grandchild, a gift from God and I feel we are going to be kindred spirits in the Kingdom. You are my new heart and world.

Ryan, my only Son in Love, an answered prayer for my daughter. Thank you for pushing me to go for things and reach past what I think I can do.

My Parents who believed in me and cheered me on and never saw anything but good in me. I've always loved our talks about Jesus together.

Holly, my sister, what can I say? My friend, my confidant, and my everything. Thanks for being my support, editor, knowing my voice, and keeping me going through this process!

My Grandmothers, for sowing the seeds of Jesus in me as a young girl that brought forth the harvest in my life. You both had lasting impacts on me.

My pastors and friends, Christina and David Campos, who grabbed my hand and said let's go girl! Y'all have cheered me on, gotten me out of my comfort zone, and shown me how true leadership is about making room for everyone at the table! You both have servant hearts and hands. I am humbled that Jesus would allow me to run with y'all.

My best friend, Kellie, we have lived a lot of life together. Thanks for always being there and cheering me on.

My friend, Jackie, who has walked with me through this process, and cheered me on.

My One Chapel church family for being my support, encouragement, and lessons along the way. You all make my life truly blessed.

The Self-Publishing team for giving me the blueprint I needed, in order to step into something I knew nothing about. Nothing but good to say about this experience.

Deb Hall, my editor, for cleaning up my mess and cheering me on—you are a delight to know.

Karen Pina, my writing coach, for holding me accountable and keeping me going in the right direction with wisdom and clarity. You're a true powerhouse for the Kingdom.

Hank, my German Shepherd, the only dog I've ever loved. Thank you for your constant companionship as I penned these words.

PLEASE REVIEW ON AMAZON

Hey Friends, thanks so much for reading my first book! I'd love for you to help me get this book to as many readers as possible. How can you help? Leave a review on Amazon and tell why you loved this book. Also, share about my book on your socials, buy a copy for a friend and start a connect group and read it together.

Thank You!

Please take two minutes now to leave a helpful review on Amazon letting me know what you thought of the book so others can read too:

www.truthfreedomministry.com/unthinkable

Thanks so much!

-Heather Bradley